BASIC FRENCH COOKING

LEN DEIGHTON

BASIC FRENCH COOKING

including chapters on

L'ART CULINAIRE, LES VIANDES, LES FROMAGES,
LES CORPS GRAS, LA CARTE DES VINS,
LA CUISINE FRANÇAISE ET LE FROID, LE LEXIQUE,
LA BATTERIE DE CUISINE

and

50 COOKSTRIPS 50

Revised and enlarged from *Où est le garlic*

CREATIVE ARTS BOOK COMPANY • BERKELEY

This is a new edition of the book
published by Jonathan Cape Ltd.

Creative Arts edition published 1987.

For information contact:
Creative Arts Book Company
833 Bancroft Way
Berkeley, California 94710

ISBN 0-88739-020-X

Library of Congress Catalog Card No. 87-70507

Printed in the United States of America

Acknowledgments and Note

The cookstrips were not originally devised for publication. When I was studying illustration at the Royal College of Art and spending my vacation time working in restaurants I found these sketch-notes a useful way of pinning up in the kitchen the essential facts of a recipe. And it kept my cookery books free of gravy spots and loose flour.

It was Clive Irving and Ray Hawkey who suggested that such notes could be used as a newspaper cookery column. Ray Hawkey designed the first one with black grid and cartoon lettering done by lettering artist Bill Harmer and it was published in the *Observer*. With pleasure I reprint my original thanks to the people concerned, especially George Seddon, John Lucas and most particularly my friend John Marshal, who often helped with the art-work. A selection of these cookstrips was later published by Jonathan Cape under the title *Action Cook Book*. It is now out of print.

My great interest in French cooking prompted me to work on a long-term project in which the fundamental facts of French cooking could be explained in no more than fifty strips. As a guiding principle I concentrated on the sort of dishes one would hope to find in a small French country restaurant. The result was the fifty strips published here. An enthusiastic response from readers of the *Observer* was followed by publication as a Penguin book. The original designer — a French graphic artist named Jacques Dehornois — was taken ill during the planning of the book, and my very old friend Ray Hawkey once again stepped in and rescued the whole project. For this, and countless other favours, I welcome this chance to thank him again. I must also record the work done at Penguin Books by the late Tony Richardson and the late Tony Godwin.

When Penguin Books allowed *Où est le garlic* to go out of print, there being no hardback edition in any country, it was not available anywhere, until that lively New York City newspaper *Village Voice* published an article about the world's finest cookery books. Alex Szogyi chose *Où est le garlic* as 'one of the best arranged and explicated works on French cuisine.' I am most indebted to him for this kind and generous verdict, on the strength of which Harper & Row, in particular Frances Lindley, decided to publish a hardback American edition. A British hardback edition soon followed. For this new Jonathan Cape edition I thank Anton Felton — my alter ego — and at Cape Tom Maschler.

Minor changes for the American edition gave me a chance to reconsider the whole text. There was little to be added or taken away but I hope that by means of a number of small alterations I have clarified certain things. At home a copy of this book is never far from the stove and we use the margins and inside covers as a place to jot notes, cooking times and ideas. Many of these too have been incorporated and for her contribution I must thank my wife Ysabele. Thanks also to an unsung army of guests — and my family — who have nibbled politely at my failures and said:

'No, really, I *like* it like that!'

TABLE DES MATIÈRES

TABLE DES MATIÈRES

INTRODUCTION

My mother – who was once a professional cook – encouraged me to help her in the kitchen from the time when I was very small. To her I owe everything. Nowadays we encourage our own little boys in the same way.

I was about sixteen when I scraped together enough money to go alone to Paris, and eat a meal at the Tour d'Argent. An American, passing my table as he left, said, 'My wife and I had to tell you that we've never seen anyone looking so happy in all our lives.'

During six years studying art I spent most of my vacation time working in the kitchens of good restaurants. I've never ceased to be interested in cooking, and in the skill that contributes to the success of a great restaurant (and that by definition means a restaurant in France).

The importance of French cookery is not only due to the taste, texture and appearance of the resulting dishes, but also to the systematic way in which generations of cooks have ordered and classified their knowledge.

This book is not a recipe book, it's a carefully planned course that has already taught many men and women to cook. The first half consists of lessons in theory, from choosing a saucepan and a cheese to pronouncing and translating a French menu. The second half of the book contains fifty practical cooking lessons in easy to follow cookstrip form. Each lesson illustrates a technique, a process or a category of dish. Most recipes have been chosen because they also provide the cook with dozens – in some cases hundreds – of variations, for instance *soufflé*, *crêpes* and *mousse*.

This is not a 'creative cookery' course; there are no concoctions of mine here. This book is the result of years of watching, and talking with, fine chefs and trying out their recipes. Here I have explained them as simply as possible. In order to fit a complete course of cookery into one slim volume I have assumed that you are intelligent and interested in cooking. No more than this is needed.

You may feel that some of my distinctions are dogmatic. Cooks are seldom dogmatic, feeling – rightly – more interested in results than in rules. But distinc-

tions exist so that the reasoning behind the methods is easily understood and remembered. Obviously it doesn't affect me if you fry the ingredients of a *daube* or a *blanquette*, but ask me why this is not called *braiser* and *fricasser* and I'd have no answer.

This, then, is Basic French Cooking. I can only tell you the rules of the game; you are the best judge of when to stick to them.

LEN DEIGHTON

L'ART CULINAIRE

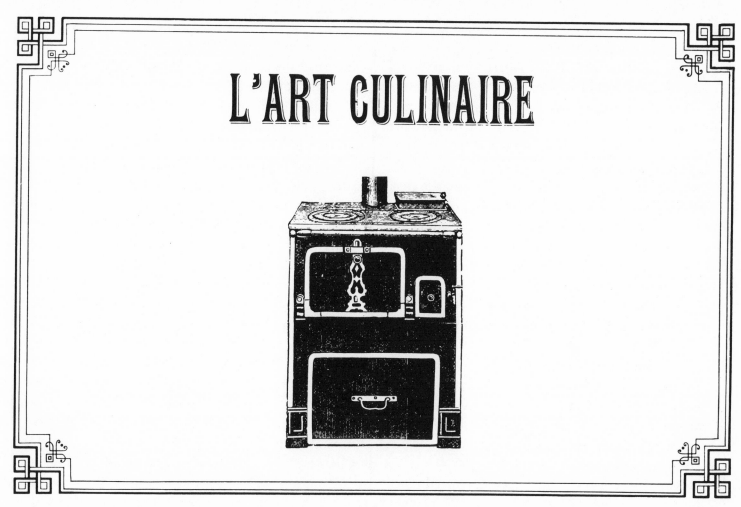

Europe has two distinct types of climate; a north suited to the production of fine cream and dairy produce, excellent beef and wonderful bacon; and a south that produces olives for olive oil, vines for wine of all kinds, luscious southern fruits, vegetables and sea food. France is the only country in Europe that includes both types of climate, and therefore has a range of foodstuffs second to none.

Because of this concern and pride in food the cook in France finds preparing a hasty meal considerably simpler than anyone in England does. For instance, the *charcuterie* will provide superb *terrines*, *pâtés*, *andouillettes*, game pies, calf's head *vinaigrette*, pork brawn, ham, cooked pork loin and *quiches*. None of these items could possibly be confused with the oddments that bear the same names as they gather dust on English grocery counters. Giving any of the latter to guests would be a most unfriendly gesture.

In France the *pâtisserie* will sell cakes, flans and *vol-au-vent* cases of which no host need feel ashamed. The bread will be real and not the squashy, wrapped rubbish that is sold here in such abundance and which even restaurants unblushingly serve.

Buying is the basis of good cooking. In a French kitchen the *chef de cuisine* is the boss. He makes the menus, fixes the prices, prods the beans and puts a fingernail in the garlic. He hires the staff and dominates the kitchen.

Ideally in an old-fashioned French kitchen the tasks are carefully assigned. The sauce chef – *chef saucier* – is the senior man in the kitchen after the *chef de cuisine*. There is also a fish chef – *chef poissonnier*; a soup chef – *chef potager*; and a chef in charge of vegetables, eggs and sweets who for complex historic reasons is called a *chef entremettier*. The man supervising the grills, roasts, and frying is a *rôtisseur* but if the menu includes many fried foods there may be a *friturier* to do the frying. It's also possible that there will be a *grillardin* for the grill, a *chef pâtissier* for the desserts of all kinds and perhaps even a *chef cafetier* for the tea and coffee. The *garde-manger* not only guards the larders and refrigerators but is also in charge of preparations of cold dishes – *pâtés*, *terrines* and *aspics*. Each chef has assistants called *commis*, some may have three. You are going to do all these tasks; it's a tricky job but relax, you aren't directing a battle. Even if the meal is a write-off your guests will put up with it if you stay in a good mood.

Remember that no professional chef tackles some complex new dish when preparing a banquet. He cooks the dishes he's mastered. Do the same and save your experiments for the family.

The kitchen must be well organized. Working surfaces should be wood, kept clear and clean. Keep dishes clean and knives sharp. Put things in the same place always. Throw away gadgets you don't use, they are just collecting dust. Wear an apron if you like, but in any case have a belt into which you can tuck a clean cloth. It will save you time and temper looking for it.

There are many types of pots and pans available. The heaviest, thickest metal ones are best for all-round cooking. The mass of metal holds the heat and spreads it evenly. Thin metal will bend and burn. Cooking in a thin frying-pan is the most difficult culinary task I can think of; a professional wouldn't even try it. It's better to use a heavy saucepan for deep-frying than a cheap thin metal deep-fryer. Earthenware pots are excellent for more gentle cooking methods, especially in the oven. Some recipes depend upon keeping as much moisture as possible in the pot. For these you should use cooking pots that have no air vents in the lids.

But a vital part of the cook's *batterie* is an understanding of what is happening to the food as the heat is applied to it. Without this even the finest recipe is just mumbo-jumbo. The cook uses what he has. Some cooks may have a great variety of cooking devices; others only a gas ring. I have listed ten basic types of heat so that you can compare them and see that the process of cooking food has simple, sensible rules. A recipe – if it is a good one – follows these same rules no matter what is being cooked. Heat can be the simple radiant heat of an open fire or grill, the semi-dry heat of an oven, the wet heat of a *braisière*, the heated water of poaching, steam in a steamer, super-heated steam in a pressure cooker, a hot frying-pan or deep fat. Each of these ways of heating food will be mentioned later, but first let's take a look at the food, the things subjected to these varying types of heat.

ANIMAL FIBRES

Meat, fish, and poultry are the basic protein foods. All protein hardens if cooked above boiling point, so the only protein foods cooked at high temperature are the expensive, tender cuts that will tolerate it. These foods dry when heated and since the juice inside is the source of their flavour the cook's task is to minimize that drying. The first step should be to persuade guests to have their beef underdone. Pork is unsafe to eat if not completely cooked, but don't make this a reason for drying it to a crisp. It should be moist inside. (To be unsafe to eat, it has to be below 131° F. which is pinker and more raw than a bloody – *saignant* – steak.)

Egg and fish are also protein foods but they are much softer than meat, so although they will harden above boiling point they will not be rendered inedible. But a fresh new-laid egg will still taste better cooked below boiling point than above. An egg that's not new-laid will taste disgusting no matter what you do with it. Eggs subjected to brisk heat (e.g. omelette) are best served only partly cooked, i.e. still moist and soft in the centre.

FAT

Fat occurs naturally in animal tissue. When meat is heated the fat melts and becomes dripping. Dripping always has a great deal of flavour so the cook uses it with care. There are all kinds of refined fats on the market: vegetable fats, vegetable oils, olive oil and butter. When fat is used as part of the texture of food, e.g. rubbed into pastry, cake mixtures, sponge, etc., the cook is most concerned with its flavour, but when the fat is used as a cooking medium – frying and sautéing – then the choice is based upon the temperature at which it burns. Even the fat which burns most easily – butter – can go much hotter than boiling water. On page 112 I have listed the burning points of various fats so you can compare them with the boiling point of water. N.B. When you are cooking in butter its burning point can be raised by adding a little oil.

FLOUR

When heat is applied to flour it goes hard. Very, very hard. If you mix flour and water and then cook it, it will become rock-like, so the cook makes sure that things made with flour have plenty of tiny air particles in them.

The glutens in flour which produce the starch provide the cook with a binding – *liaison* – an ingredient that will thicken liquids. If you stir a little cold water into an ounce of flour and go on pouring and stirring until you have half a pint of mixture you will have made a *liaison à la meunière*. If you apply heat to it, it will begin to thicken – keep stirring and don't let it boil. After three minutes' simmering the flour will have glutenized, it will be as thick as it gets and the floury taste will have disappeared. You have made a sauce. It won't be a very interesting sauce, but if you had used flavoured water or even milk it would have been a real sauce.

Because fat can be made much hotter than water the cook usually glutenizes the flour in butter and then adds the water or etc. This combination of fat + flour is called a *roux*; it's described further on pages 118–19 and 128–9.

SUGAR

Sugar caramelizes when heated. It turns a golden yellow, then light brown and, according to the amount of heat you apply, eventually black and burned.

VEGETABLES

Vegetables soften when heated by the cook. They don't contain protein so you can boil them furiously if you want to. Frying is hotter than boiling and so when you fry vegetables you will see the sugar in them caramelize. Fried onions will, with a little heat, lose their capacity for making your eyes water, then they will soften and after that go a golden colour, then brown. Now they have taken on quite a different flavour. The cook sometimes uses this caramelization of onions etc. to add flavour and/or colour to a stew.

EGG

Egg is protein. All protein hardens above boiling point. Although egg is often given a blast of fierce heat we always make sure that it's only partly cooked. Omelettes, scrambled eggs, poached eggs, boiled eggs are given just enough heat to make them firm. Cook them longer and you'll find yourself in the plastics industry.

High temperature releases hydrogen sulphide (from the sulphur in the egg-white) and makes an egg taste stale. This same sulphur combines with iron in the yolk to make that grey ring round the yolk of a hard-boiled egg that has been made too hot. So you see that a real boiled egg is unattractive, indigestible and tastes disgusting.

Although a 'boiled egg' goes into boiling water, do not reheat it to boiling point. Keep the water well below boiling temperature so that the surface just moves (the French say *frémir* which means to shiver and perfectly describes it). The water is now at about 185° F.

The most satisfactory way to cook the egg in its shell is the old-fashioned method of 'coddling'. Bring a pint of water to the maximum boil. This rolling confusion of water, changing to steam, is nearly at 212° F. Put one egg into the water, put a lid on the saucepan and turn off the heat. After approximately six minutes, eat it. I say approximately because the freshness of the egg influences the cooking time, and you might need to modify your cooking times to find the right one for your eggs, and your taste. Measure the amount of water you use, and provide one pint of water per egg. And from now onwards, remember how to estimate water temperature.

The egg is also a *liaison*, used, as flour is, to bind liquids into a sauce. But while flour is tough enough to withstand boiling, the protein of the egg curdles at 167° F., and your sauce collapses. So when there is egg in your sauce be cautious. Heat it gently, and if possible cook it in a double boiler (a basin over a saucepan of water will do). But there is a way of cheating – add a trace of flour to the egg and the sauce will withstand boiling, if you bring it to the boil slowly.

ALCOHOL

When wine or spirits are used in cooking they must be subjected to considerable heat or they will be very indigestible. Unless alcohol is set on fire, or has over one hour's cooking at any temperature, it should be boiled until half its bulk has evaporated.

WATER

Water is perhaps the most important of all things subjected to the heat of cooking because all foods contain water. About 60 per cent of the weight of meat is water. Fish is 65–80 per cent water and vegetables and fruit 85–95 per cent water. (Foods that don't contain water, e.g. dried fish, dried peas and beans, rice, etc., won't go bad, because the bacteria in water cause that, but they will need water added to them again before being cooked.)

When water is added to food mixtures – especially those containing flour – the amount of water is very important. Any sort of pastry must have only enough water added to make the mixture manageable. Batter mixtures should be like cream. Cake mixtures are somewhere between the two. The difficulty for people writing recipes is that flour varies in its absorbency. And because flour absorbs water, batter mixtures left to stand will thicken.

Thirdly, water is used as a cooking medium. As well as being cheap, it won't heat beyond 212° F. What's more, when it gets near that temperature it will bubble and steam, so the cook has a constant visual check on the temperature.

AIR

Air expands when it's heated. Cooks use this fact in many cooking processes in order to get a texture of holes through the food. Pastry would be a concrete slab and steamed puddings solid rubber if it wasn't for the tiny particles of air that had expanded to raise the texture. Remember this when handling various types of mixture. Everything must be cold when handling pastry – some cooks chill the dough – so that the cold air will expand more. Pastry must not be carelessly handled, or the air particles will be lost. When stiffly beaten egg-whites are folded into a mixture the word 'fold' is used to emphasize the gentle way the bubbles must be handled. Wet mixtures for cakes are beaten like mad to get air into them. Batter mixtures are best if beaten just before cooking.

Self-raising flour has bicarbonate of soda – a raising agent – added to it to produce bubbles. Beating such mixtures can reduce the effectiveness of the raising agent. Yeast does exactly the same (although, because oven heat halts the action of the yeast, the raising takes place in a warm kitchen before the actual cooking).

METHODS OF COOKING

Having dealt with the types of foodstuffs available, let's turn on the heat.

DRY RADIANT HEAT

Dry radiant heat of open fire, barbecue fire, domestic grill, or broiler. This is the most basic sort of cooking heat there is. It uses open radiant heat (as against the enclosed moister heat of an oven). Although this is a favourite way of cooking meat it is something of an abuse. Only first quality cuts, that will be tender under any circumstances, can be cooked this way. The object is to keep as much moisture and flavour in the meat as possible and to avoid drying the meat right through. For that reason the best things to grill are the things that you like to eat with an under-cooked centre, e.g. steak, beef hamburgers, and toasted bread. Things that must be cooked right through, e.g. pork chops, fish, and veal, have to be moved a little farther away from the heat source or they'll be burned outside before they are completely cooked.

There is an old French saying that a chef is made but a *grillardin* is born. Grilling requires constant attention because half a minute too long means disaster when the heat is so great. The meat or fish is usually painted with a trace of oil; grilling is especially suited to foods that already contain a lot of fat, e.g. streaky bacon or any oily type of fish.

Since fat shrinks at a faster rate than lean meat it is usual to slash the fat around a piece of steak (see page 188) to prevent the meat curling up. A professional cook taps the meat to test it; meat hardens as it cooks. It's impossible to give times of cooking because I don't know how much heat your grill produces nor how far away from it the food is. Always have the grill very hot; light it ten minutes before use if electric or gas. Make sure the grill pan is also very hot. On my grill a half-inch thick steak takes four minutes per side while a steak one-and-a-half inches thick takes more like eight minutes per side. A half *poussin* takes about thirty-five minutes but is farther away. A one-inch thick fish steak takes five minutes per side and a herring split open takes about five minutes, after which serve it without turning it over.

SEMI-DRY HEAT

Semi-dry heat of oven. When a piece of meat is two inches thick it's too big to put under a normal-size grill. In olden days they roasted a whole ox in the open but only by having a vast heat source. Nowadays we use an oven because that encloses the heat around the food and so costs less in fuel and takes up less space. But the enclosed space means that the hot air will become moist, because the water inside the meat is turning to steam. The old open-fire method of cooking – roasting – was so dry that it needed an attendant who would watch the spit turning and constantly moisten the outside of the meat with fat. We still do this when we brush fat over a steak before grilling, because that's radiant heat, but when a joint is put in an oven there is no need to baste it. In fact basting the meat is THE WORST THING YOU CAN DO TO IT. Since there is no need to baste it there is no need to have the meat standing in a tray of highly indigestible burning fat. I will explain why.

All meat shrinks when subjected to heat. Because the meat contains juice, that juice will be forced to the surface by the shrinkage. The juice is vital and everything must be done to preserve it. The hot air of the oven will dry those juices as they emerge and the outside of the meat will be dark and shiny. That first outside slice will be delicious. If you baste the meat you are rinsing those juices away as fast as the heat dries them; stop it. In fact, do the reverse, sprinkle a trace of flour over the raw joint to encourage the juices to dry as they emerge. While the joint is cooking don't prod the meat, and especially don't stick a fork into it or a stream of juice will escape.

Fat is an important part of cooking; it should occur naturally in the tissue of the meat but you can put it there by sewing threads – *lardons* – through it or putting thin sheets of fat around it (pages 176–9 and 186–7 illustrate this). Having done that, put the meat on a wire rack so that the heat can get all around it. Put it in the oven. When it is ready, eat it. When is it ready?

Cooking means bringing the centremost part to a certain temperature. If you have a meat thermometer the sensitive point of it will register this temperature. Leave the thermometer in the joint until the meat is done. If you have a glass-fronted oven you can watch the temperature rise. These are the temperatures I recommend, although the beef and mutton might be a little too underdone for some tastes. Remember though that it's the underdone meat that contains the most flavourful juices. The temperatures I have given for pork and veal are generally agreed to be the best ones; these meats are never eaten underdone (i.e. never below 131° F.).

	° F.		° F.
Lamb	165	Beef underdone	140
Mutton	145	Beef medium	160
Pork	180	Veal	175

If you don't have a thermometer then it's usual to guess the time the meat will take to cook by weighing the joint while considering its general shape, e.g. a thin flat-shaped piece will cook more quickly than a cube shape. As for grilling, only the better quality cuts of beef are suitable for roasting although, because a pig doesn't get so muscular, any part of a pig can be roasted and very nearly any cut of veal or lamb, if you are careful (i.e. don't have the oven heat too high). The general heat for cooking meat is 350–400° F. because that's hot enough to ensure the meat doesn't generate too much steam, but if you have a

meat thermometer and like your beef crusty outside and juicy inside you can step up the heat. Cooking inside an oven is called baking. The roast beef of old England is more correctly called the baked beef of old England but the two words have become interchangeable because nowadays no one does true roasting. For some things this semi-dry heat in a box is particularly good, e.g. fish, pastry, bread, and cakes. What's more, an enclosed box of heat can be measured and controlled.

Many flour mixtures have finished cooking when they become quite dry and so recipes tell you to insert a long needle; if it comes out with a trace of wet mixture on it the cooking isn't completed. Leave such tests until as near the end of the process as you can. Opening the oven door before the flour has had a chance to harden will result in the tiny particles of heated air that are holding it all up cooling and collapsing: cake sinks.

Thermometers are used only in meat cookery; other items are given the time stated by the recipe plus the skill and experience of the cook. I suggest you make a mark in the margin of the recipe so that next time you will know the exact time that suits your oven. Baked goods are usually allowed to cool on a wire rack so that the steam can escape from all sides and not be trapped and cause sogginess. Meat too will be easier to carve if it is rested – *reposé* – for ten or fifteen minutes in a warm place, but remember that the cooking process will continue inside the meat even after it's come out of the oven. Allow for that.*

* If letting meat rest for 15 mins, remove it from oven 10 mins before it's due to be ready (if using meat thermometer, remove joint to warm place when it's still 10° F. below desired temperature).

SAUTER

Sauter means to cook in a frying pan with just enough fat to prevent the food sticking. Originally the food was turned by tossing it (*sauter* means to jump); so you see the fat must be minimal. Food to be cooked in this way is usually in thin slices (i.e. slices of veal or calf liver) although sometimes larger things are sautéed for a few minutes to brown them before cooking them in liquid. Onions, carrots, and pieces of meat are often treated like this before they are put in a stew. This is because oil can be heated far beyond the boiling point of water; when we want to extract flavours only available at high temperature this is

how it's done. Fish is often sautéed because its flesh cooks quickly. If the fish has a heavy skin, remove the skin before cooking. If it has a light skin the chef often makes shallow diagonal cuts along the fish to help the heat enter – this is called scotching; it also helps to prevent the fish curling, for all flesh foods shrink when heated and some distort (see also *meunière*, pages 168–9 and *sauté*, pages 180–1).

FRITURE

The word frying – *friture* – means just one thing in France. It means what we call deep-frying, a technique introduced into Britain and the U.S.A. in comparatively recent times. That's why in America deep-fried potatoes are called 'French fries'. The secret of *friture* is cleanliness of pan and fat and what one expert calls 'surprise': the immersing of the item of food in the fat in one fast movement. The fat must always be deep so that the piece of food can float in the fat. The fat must not be old or burnt and if the frying is done correctly there should be no taste of fat in the fried food. The French chef would probably use rendered down beef suet – the fat around the beef kidney – for all kinds of deep-frying (although, of course, he would have a separate pan of it for cooking fish). Vegetable oils are good, especially for sweet items. Mutton fat is never used. Butter burns too easily and is too expensive, and veal fat goes bad too quickly. The technique depends upon the temperature being kept high but never so high that the fat burns. (A thermostat-controlled pan is valuable for deep-frying.) Use a large pan with plenty of fat in it and don't cram the food in. If you drop a large piece of food into a small pan of fat the temperature will drop. So keep the pieces of food small and of the same size. You must cook the centre before the outside goes dark and overdone.

Since the fat will be well above the boiling point of water any water inside deep-fried food will boil and then turn to steam. For instance, the water inside a potato chip will steam-cook the inside and then bubble up through the fat. This expanding steam keeps the fat at bay; if it didn't the fat would invade the food and make it greasy and unpleasant. The raw piece of potato must be carefully dried or else so many bubbles of steam will come up that the fat will spill over the side of the pan. Also any water on the potato will be cold; it will lower the temperature of the fat. So the two basic rules are: keep the fat hot and the food dry.

The moisture inside a piece of potato is water, so it doesn't matter if it escapes into the fat, but the moisture inside meat is juice which will burn if it escapes into the very hot fat. In any case we can't afford to lose that juice. The answer is to create a barrier that will keep the juice inside. Flour makes a good barrier and if you dip the food (e.g. fish) into milk first it will help the flour cling. This coating is called *fariner*.

A more complex coating – *paner à l'anglaise* – is a dip into flour, then beaten egg, and after that tiny breadcrumbs are pressed on to the food. This is often used with fish and liver.

Perhaps the best barrier of all, especially for fragile foods or juicy foods like raw meat, is a simple batter (use recipe on page 160, but make it a little thicker so it's like heavy cream).

As I have said, in France food is either sautéed with an absolute minimum of fat or deep-fried. A fried egg would be deep-fried in France. If you think that's crazy, watch yourself next time you are throwing spoonfuls of fat over the top of an egg while it's frying. If you want to do deep-fat frying – and it's by no means essential – then it will cost you time, trouble and money. Keep the pan clean and the fat filtered through a cloth between each batch of cooking. Store the fat in the cool when it's not in use. Darkened oil has been used enough – throw it away. Fat that has been burned must be thrown away.

Still not discouraged? Then here's some last advice. Deep-fried food tastes best if served immediately after cooking. Put it on hot plates and don't put a lid over it because the hot air trapped around the food will make the crisp coating go limp. Absorbent paper will remove excess fat from the surface of the food before it goes to the table.

THOSE first four methods of cookery are suited to meat that will be served with its centre underdone (i.e. first-quality cuts and finely chopped meat). The following cooking methods are for cheaper cuts that will be served cooked right through.

VERY MOIST HEAT

In English cookery there is a method of cooking meat called 'pot-roasting'. Its equivalent in French cooking is braising. A piece of meat is put inside a close-fitting pot with a heavy lid (the lid has no air vent). Little or no moisture is added but usually there are some vegetables. Heat is applied to the pot by any means you like; this causes the moisture inside the raw food to turn into steam and this cooks the food. If you are applying heat from underneath the pot you will have to turn the contents over every half an hour because the food will be hotter at the bottom. So it's better to put the whole pot inside an oven where there's no need to turn the contents over because the heat is all around the pot. Whatever sort of heat you apply it will have to be gentle or else you will dry up all the moisture in the food and burn it. (Originally the pot had hot ashes and charcoal heaped upon it.) Pot-roasted joints are usually cheaper foods, such as boiling-chicken or topside of beef which are eaten well cooked. For best results keep the oven temperature very low, i.e. not above 300° F. (Reg. $1\frac{1}{2}$), and allow a long cooking time.

Most cooks put a large knob of fat into the pot and fry the outside of the meat to make it brown before beginning to cook it. A few large chunks of onion or carrot provide extra moisture and extra flavour. For a more complex addition try the *mirepoix* described on pages 120–1. The French cook will always be very attentive when cooking in this way. He looks into the pot and dribbles a spoonful of stock over the meat. The meat must never stand in a pool of water or stock, it must be moist enough and hot enough to make its own steam. Maximum amount of basting with the minimum amount of liquid is the rule. See pages 184–5, and, for vegetables braised, pages 196–7.

Another way of using this same technique is to wrap a piece of food in heavy paper (or the transparent plastic 'roasting bag') and put it into a gentle oven. This food too cooks in its own moist heat. This is called cooking *en papillotes* and is described on pages 170–1.

STEWING

This is cooking done by circulating liquid. The liquid circulates because the pot is standing upon heat which causes the heated water to rise, move around, and cook the whole thing evenly by convection. Usually the food is cut into pieces because that speeds the process and releases more flavour into the liquid. (In this cooking method it doesn't matter if flavour escapes from the meat.) Sometimes the meat is left in one large piece but as long as the liquid is free to circulate, it's a stew. Fricassée, pages 182–3, is a stew. A heavy thickened mixture in which the liquid does not circulate is not a stew, it is braising and should be cooked in the oven.

Stews can be solely protein foods, e.g. chicken, beef, fish, or veal, or can have vegetables such as carrots, potato, and onion added to them during the last part of the cooking time so it will all be ready together. In any case stews must be cooked slowly and gently – *faire cuire doucement* – and never be allowed to boil or bubble. About 180° F. (far below Reg. $\frac{1}{4}$) is ideal. Keep meat pieces equal size then they'll all take the same time to cook. Total weight of meat used makes no difference, it's the size of the cubes that counts. Leg of beef, the cheapest cut there is, will need about four hours; chuck steak, a medium-price cut, a little over two hours. The cheaper cut will be better flavoured and the streaks of connective tissue, which look horrible when you are cutting it up, will dissolve with long cooking and become a rich gravy. This body or texture – *du corps* – of the stew is a sign of a cook's skill. Some cooks try to get it by artificial means, e.g. stirring in a little flour or a little potato that goes mashy. That's terrible, try to avoid it. Get the texture by ingredients. For extra body add something that will give you texture, e.g. veal knuckle, pig's foot, chicken feet, tripe, or oxtail, then discard it before serving.

It's usual to add some flavouring matter to the stew liquid; onion, garlic, herbs, bacon, or ham. If you fry such items in olive oil the heat will bring out the flavour and the oil will add one of its own.* For a stronger flavour, part of the liquid is sometimes replaced by wine. Sometimes the cook is only concerned with the flavour of the liquid, intending to discard the meat finally and use only the stock. If you compare pages 128 and 130 you will see that the only difference between the finest way of making stock and the classic recipe for the French dish *pot-au-feu* is that in the latter you use a better-looking cut of meat.

In these notes about stewing I have concentrated on meat, but fish makes wonderful stews. Mix various types of sea fish to make *bouillabaisse* and various types of fresh-water fish to make *matelote*. If you are inventing a stew, beware of oily types of fish. Put the softest sort of fish pieces in last because they will cook more quickly. For best results have a little of various kinds. In any case fish stews will cook in less than half an hour, so go ahead, there's time to invent a stew.

BOILING AND POACHING

Both words mean cooking in water on top of the stove, but the temperatures are different. The French are more precise in their words: when water is heated enough to shiver – *frémir* – it is just right for poaching – *pocher*; when it gets hotter there will be a bubble now and again at the same place. That is called *mijoter* and as far as the cook is concerned the water is boiling. (Beware, the cook seldom wants anything boiling.) If the water gets very hot it will go into a great rolling boil – *bouillir* – which is fine for reducing the volume of liquids but not for very much else.

Many dishes are called boiled but very few are actually boiled. (This word usually indicates that the liquid in which the food is cooked will not be served with it, i.e. boiled bacon, boiled mutton, etc.) Food-stuffs that are actually put into boiling water include

* Technically all stews that have ingredients fried first are called fricassées.

eggs in their shells, vegetables, dried vegetables, cereals, and a few flour mixtures like *pasta*, suet puddings, and dumplings. Of these only the last wouldn't be just as good if cooked more slowly. (That's because there are air particles which must be kept hot or they will collapse just as in baking pastry or cake.)

Most foods are best poached, i.e. kept at that gentle simmer or *frémir* as in poaching an egg. In English cookery it is very often the salt meats that are cooked in this way: salt beef, salt pork, bacon, and ham; that's because immersion in water takes some of the salt taste out of them. Originally such foods were salted for the winter as a way of preserving them. By the time they were used they were very salty and needed a soaking in cold water before they were cooked. If you take my mother's excellent advice about salt meat you will choose a suitable piece of meat and then ask your butcher to salt it in his brine tub. This will take about three days. After this brief salting it shouldn't need any soaking, just go ahead and cook it. Don't buy salt meat at random from the brine tub because the butcher sometimes consigns his old unsold meat to it and if it's been in there too long it will be excessively salty. The standard rule for cooking salt meat: twenty-five minutes per pound plus twenty-five minutes. However I find that long cooking improves it and I suggest a four-hour minimum for any piece. You need a pan big enough for the meat to just float and the water to circulate freely.

The French cook is not fond of salt meat; perhaps that has something to do with having a less severe winter and therefore not having to slaughter the animals at the winter solstice. More likely it's because the liquid in which salt meat has been cooked is quite unusable as stock. With unsalted meat, however, the cooking liquid is served alongside as a soup; see *pot-au-feu* (page 130). Clever frugal French. There's more about poaching on pages 174–5.

CUISSON AU BAIN MARIE

If you put a basin of water inside a saucepan of boiling water, you will find it very difficult to bring the water in the basin to the boil, no matter how furiously you heat the saucepan. The basin will remain at the same temperature, 180°–90° F., which is right for most cookery; so you can braise, poach, or stew using this type of gadget. All the double-boiler does is make braising, poaching, or stewing easier. It's a way of cooking delicate mixtures, e.g. egg custard and those sort of thick stews that are too solid to circulate (that *daube* on page 186 would be too solid). In fact that type of stew is commonly called a hot-pot because it stands in a saucepan of water. The *terrine* on page 172 is also a type of double-boiler.

This is one of the most perfect ways of cooking. It requires very little attention – just making sure the saucepan doesn't boil dry – and because the rate of cooking is slow the time factor isn't too vital. Sometimes the inner container has a tight-fitting lid. (In the case of apple pudding and steak pudding the food is encased and sealed in suet pastry.) Because blood, being protein, curdles at 176° F. this is the way jugged hare must be cooked. Superior types of stew can be cooked this way, so can eggs *en cocotte* (page 158); in fact anything can be cooked this way, even large pieces of meat. A piece of meat weighing three pounds – and I doubt if you will find a double-boiler to hold anything bigger than this – will need at least four hours but an extra hour won't spoil it.

Some ovens can be adjusted to give heat below the boiling point of water – 212° F. – and obviously a pot put inside such an oven will get exactly the same sort of heat as a double-boiler. Such cooking is called *étuver*.

STEAMING

The process of steaming provides a vivid chance to see the difference between heat and temperature. Put your hand into the hot air of an oven at 212° F. and you'll feel no more than discomfort but I advise you not to plunge your hand into water that is at this (boiling) temperature. Hot water is more violent than hot air and more violent than steam. A potato cooked in the dissipated heat of a steamer will take longer to cook than one that is boiled.

Steaming is done by putting food into a perforated container and placing that over a saucepan of boiling water. Only the steam touches the food. Sometimes egg mixtures – like custards – are steamed and they are much better than the same mixture boiled. Sometimes cooks making a pudding in a basin will stand it in simmering water so that the bottom part of it cooks double-boiler method and the top – pastry – part steams. Diabolical English cunning this. (Because this is a popular way to prepare English steak and kidney pudding, cooks often say steamed when they really mean this two-part way of cooking.)

PRESSURE COOKING

Pressure cooking is a special way of cooking at high temperature (226° F.). Although it will cook fragile things, it is at its best when neither overcooking nor violent movement of air will affect the food. Soups, stocks, stews, and vegetables that will end up as a purée (e.g. swede, potato, turnip) are particularly good. So are any dried fruits or vegetables or suet puddings. A pressure cooker – *marmite à pression* – is a valuable tool for any cook who is short of time, even if it's only used to make soup and stock. Read the instruction book that comes with it.

Although I like pressure cookers it must be added that a good cook should plan in advance, and stock that has simmered for five hours without attention is scarcely more bother than a pressure cooker that needs close attention for thirty minutes. The simmered stock will be far better.

FINALLY

In the section on steaming, a paragraph or so back, I described how a steak pudding can enjoy being half steamed and half double-boiler cooked. That's a clever and logical way to cook that dish because it is two entirely different foodstuffs being cooked in a method suited to each, i.e. pudding steamed, meat double-boiler cooked. However there are many other combination methods of cooking that stem from muddled thinking and are not logical or clever. For instance, it's not logical and clever to have a joint of meat standing in a tray of fat in a hot oven: if you want it baked, then why have it in a tray of fat; if you want it fried, why have it in the oven? Another muddled cooking method is braising (see Very moist heat, page 23) which has so much moisture in it that the bottom half is stewing. Do whatever is best but not both together. Even more common is the cross between sautéing and frying. This is probably due to the popularity of eggs and bacon because the eggs are best deep-fried and the bacon is best sautéed. To save time and trouble most British cooks have their fat about an eighth of an inch deep for everything they fry. This is too shallow for cooking eggs and yet so deep that it swamps the bacon. Like most compromises it's the worst of both worlds.

Now that you know all the ways to cook you should be able to apply them to any chunk of food that stands in front of you.

A potato will lend itself to roasting or baking. Sliced up it can be sautéed, fried, put into a stew, boiled, poached, steamed, pressure-cooked, and, although it's unusual, pot-roasted or double-boiler cooked too. As long as you bear in mind the limitations of protein foods you can do anything any way. The only limit I would put upon you is that of using good quality meat for the first four heating methods — dry radiant heat, oven heat, sauté, and frying.

LES VIANDES

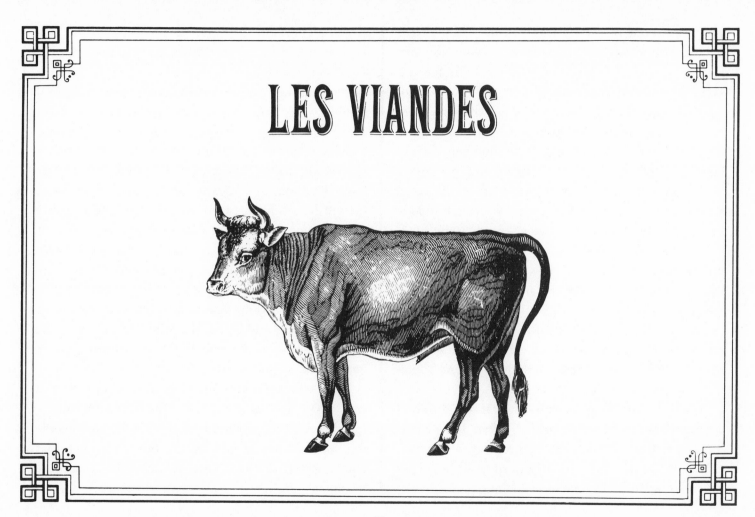

Don't ask your butcher for a small lean joint that is tender and flavourful, for they are contradictory words. Tender meat will be marbled with fat and small joints come from young animals that will not have the succulent flavour of the larger joints from more mature animals. Do not be all-demanding; tenderness isn't everything. The butcher usually bones and rolls meat on a Wednesday, so order before this if you want special cuts or meat left on the bone, which tends to be more flavourful. Most flesh food – but especially chicken and steak – needs some extra time hanging. Buy two days before you need it and unless there's a heat wave it will be O.K. at a cool room temperature. Some meats can be marinaded (see pages 186–7).

Ask for the cut you want for the recipe you will follow (recognizing the cut meat is not absolutely necessary). Don't ask for 'something to fry' or 'something to stew' – it's too vague.

American and English cuts of meat are different only in detail but French cutting differs from either in basic method. French butchers separate along each muscle while we cut up an animal as if slicing a *salame*. Therefore a Frenchman looking at one of our roasting cuts is likely to see parts of three of his cuts fastened together. So the diagrams here show not the same cut under its British name – there is no such thing although some stores now have a special butchery department that sells French-style cuts of meat – but a good substitute for it in most recipes.

What I have tried to indicate is the use a French chef would make of the animal. A French chef doesn't have the same high regard for a roast that we have, he will be attracted to the *daubes* and braised dishes that are more notable for flavour than roast meat but perhaps less attractive in appearance. Because in these latter dishes the size of the *braisière* and the *daubière* will be quite vital (the meat should fit neatly into the pot, neither pressing against the side nor leaving so much space around it that the joint will dry out), the chef in France will probably have several pots of various shapes and sizes.

Meat when put through a grinder is squeezed as well as cut. In this way a lot of the flavourful juice is lost. We tend to grin and bear this loss because grinding meat is simple and quick, but remember that cutting meat with a very sharp knife will give a more flavourful result.

The muscles that do the hardest work, e.g. leg of beef, will be the cheapest and toughest, but they will give the best flavour. Many people still believe that meat dishes can be improved by substituting more expensive cuts of meat but do not do this. Chuck is a midway cut, and therefore will need a shorter cooking period but give less good flavour. Naturally these cheaper cuts are suited only to stews and braises. A stew of leg of beef can take five hours to cook. Test for tenderness with a fork, don't let the water boil and, if it's tender before you are ready, turn off the heat and reheat it rather than serve it overcooked and 'mashy'.

Veal, mutton, pork, and lamb will seldom need more than two hours whatever the cut. Ask your butcher to put aside odd beef pieces and veal bones for a regular stock pot each week. Chicken giblets also make a good stock and can often be bought in bulk in shops selling a lot of poultry. A pound of necks and a pound of gizzards and hearts will make a fine stock. Avoid livers for stock-making, they are bitter.

BŒUF
FRENCH WAYS OF COOKING BEEF

CLOD. Stew, braise or chop finely. *Pot-au-feu*.

CHUCK. Stock, braise, stew, haché.

BRAIN. Not as good as veal brain but very good. Soak — CERVELLE
2 hours in cold water. Poach 45 mins. Serve with browned butter.

PALERON

TONGUE. Poach 3 hours, serve hot or cold. — LANGUE

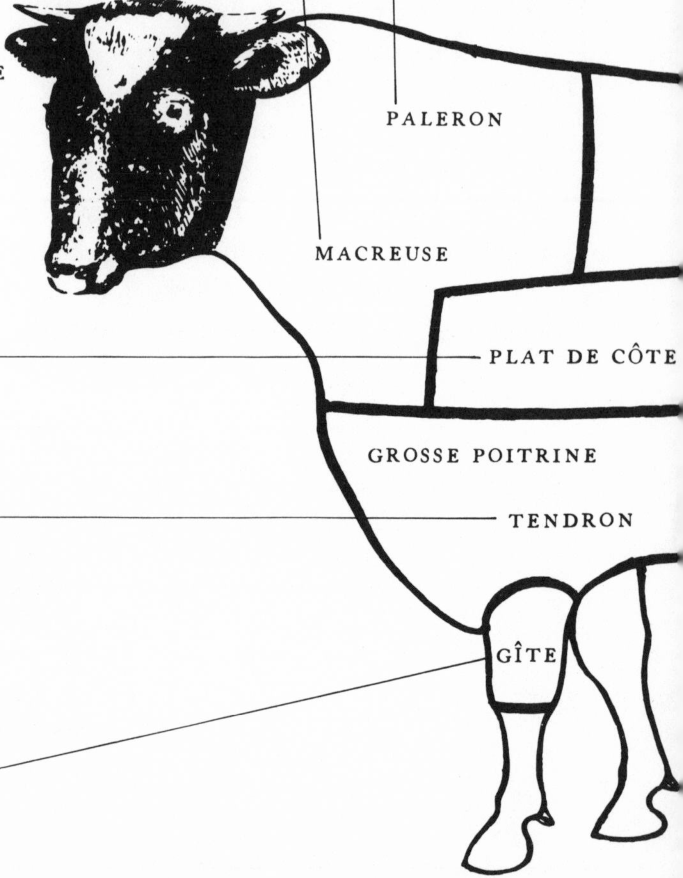

MACREUSE

FOREQUARTER FLANK. Stock. — PLAT DE CÔTE

GROSSE POITRINE

BRISKET. *Pot-au-feu* or stock (good cut for salt beef). — TENDRON

GÎTE

LEG. Just like rear leg but smaller.

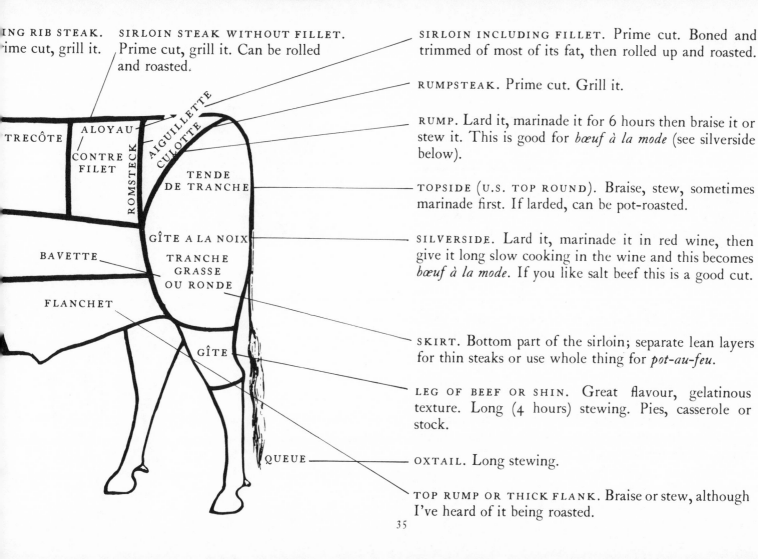

ING RIB STEAK. rime cut, grill it.

SIRLOIN STEAK WITHOUT FILLET. Prime cut, grill it. Can be rolled and roasted.

SIRLOIN INCLUDING FILLET. Prime cut. Boned and trimmed of most of its fat, then rolled up and roasted.

RUMPSTEAK. Prime cut. Grill it.

RUMP. Lard it, marinade it for 6 hours then braise it or stew it. This is good for *bœuf à la mode* (see silverside below).

TOPSIDE (U.S. TOP ROUND). Braise, stew, sometimes marinade first. If larded, can be pot-roasted.

SILVERSIDE. Lard it, marinade it in red wine, then give it long slow cooking in the wine and this becomes *bœuf à la mode*. If you like salt beef this is a good cut.

SKIRT. Bottom part of the sirloin; separate lean layers for thin steaks or use whole thing for *pot-au-feu*.

LEG OF BEEF OR SHIN. Great flavour, gelatinous texture. Long (4 hours) stewing. Pies, casserole or stock.

OXTAIL. Long stewing.

TOP RUMP OR THICK FLANK. Braise or stew, although I've heard of it being roasted.

TRECÔTE
ALOYAU
CONTRE FILET
ROMSTECK
AIGUILLETTE
CULOTTE
TENDE DE TRANCHE
GÎTE A LA NOIX
TRANCHE GRASSE OU RONDE
BAVETTE
FLANCHET
GÎTE
QUEUE

35

VEAU
FRENCH WAYS OF COOKING VEAL

French cooks prefer braising to roasting for all meat but especially for veal.

CALF'S HEAD. Buy it cleaned and blanched if possible (as Pig's Head for Brawn), serve it sliced cold with *rémoulade* or *vinaigrette* or sliced and grilled.

SCRAG (U.S. NECK). Stew it or make jellied veal (like Pig's Head Brawn recipe).

BREAST. Stew, *blanquette* or boned, stuffed and braised (with sauerkraut sometimes). This is a superb but cheap cut.

BREAST (MIDDLE CUT, U.S. RIBLETS). Contains crunchy false ribs much liked by French gourmets, but some English people don't like these sections. Slices from here can be braised slowly in butter. Can also be cut up for *blanquettes* and fricassée, etc.

SHOULDER. Meat from here plus meat from breast makes a *blanquette*. Or bone, roll and braise it. Not so good for roasting.

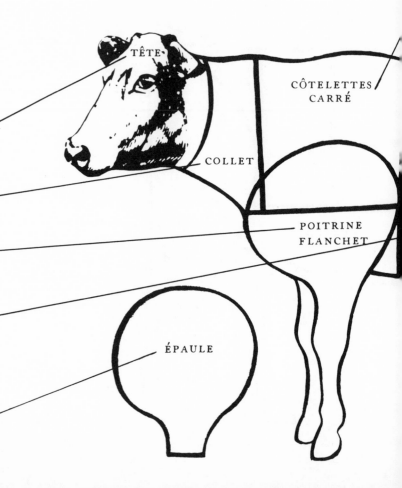

36

BEST END OF NECK (U.S. RIB ROAST). Luxury roasting joint. Cutlets from here can be sautéed or braised with tomato and onion in a covered pan.

LOIN. If roasted, boned, excess fat trimmed away but kidney remains inside, that's called a *rognonnade de veau*. If braised it can be left on the bone. A saddle (*selle*) is a double-width joint of loin.

CHUMP END OF LOIN (U.S. HEEL OR ROUND). Braise this or use it in a *daube*. Long (3–4 hours) cooking using a little dry white wine is good. Eat it hot or cold.

FILLET (U.S. ROUND ROAST). Escalope comes from this region.

TOPSIDE (U.S. RUMP). *Cuisseau* means the leg. French butchers separate 3 joints here and slice them into escalopes. These joints can be larded and braised and sometimes are served cold. Not so good for roasting.

KNUCKLE. For an unusual dish: lard it and roast it gently. Also good braised with tomatoes, garlic and onion for 2–3 hours. It's a superb thickening and enriching ingredient in any stew, e.g. beef stew, or with stuffed cabbage.

CALF'S FOOT. Great for thickening (as knuckle) and for making jelly for brawn, etc.

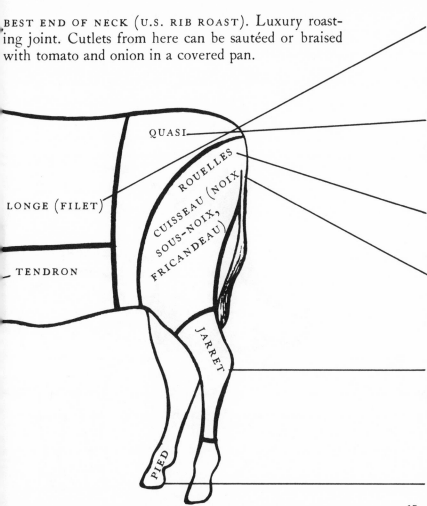

QUASI

ROUELLES

CUISSEAU (NOIX

SOUS-NOIX,

FRICANDEAU)

LONGE (FILET)

TENDRON

JARRET

PIED

PORC
FRENCH WAYS OF COOKING PORK

Any part of the pig can be roasted. Any part of the pig can be salted. If roasting it most French cooks would marinade it in any dry wine first for 3–6 hours or they might rub the meat with garlic, oil, salt and leave it overnight. Pork is particularly good when cooked in a closed pot.

ENGLISH SPARE RIB (U.S. BLADE END). Can be boned, rolled and roasted or, with all fat removed, used for *daube* or stew.

HEAD. For brawn

HAND (U.S. SHOULDER). Bone and roll it, then roast or braise. Can be boned *en daube*.

BELLY. Gives lots of good fat. Use it for *rillettes*. Can be grilled crisp like bacon in slices. Sometimes it's salted. If smoked it's bacon.

BLADEBONE (U.S. SHOULDER BUTT). Bone it and braise it, or remove fat and stew it.

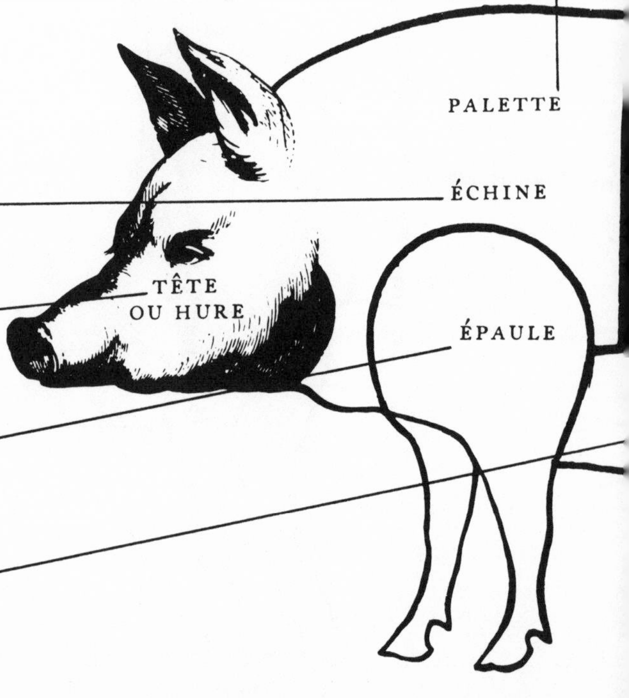

PALETTE

ÉCHINE

TÊTE OU HURE

ÉPAULE

FORE LOIN/BEST END (U.S. RIB CUT). Classic pork chop, sauté or grill them. Boned and rolled it's good braised with turnips or cabbage.

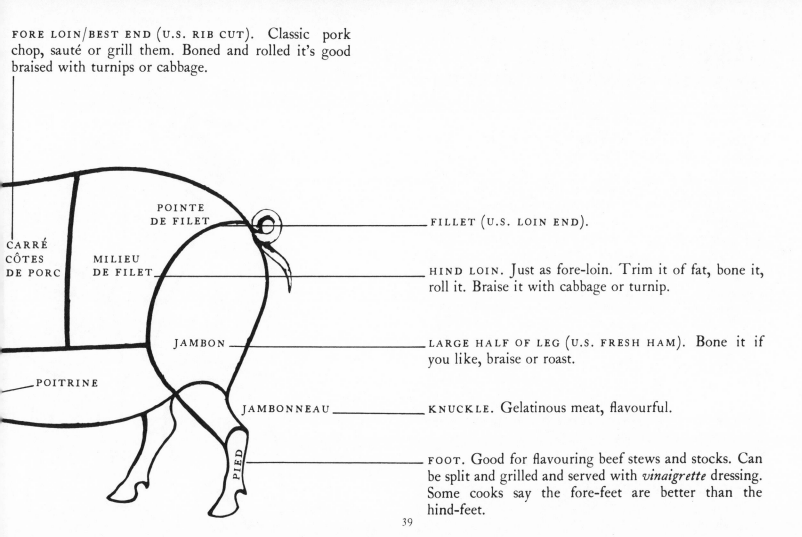

POINTE DE FILET

CARRÉ CÔTES DE PORC

MILIEU DE FILET

JAMBON

POITRINE

JAMBONNEAU

PIED

FILLET (U.S. LOIN END).

HIND LOIN. Just as fore-loin. Trim it of fat, bone it, roll it. Braise it with cabbage or turnip.

LARGE HALF OF LEG (U.S. FRESH HAM). Bone it if you like, braise or roast.

KNUCKLE. Gelatinous meat, flavourful.

FOOT. Good for flavouring beef stews and stocks. Can be split and grilled and served with *vinaigrette* dressing. Some cooks say the fore-feet are better than the hind-feet.

39

L'AGNEAU ET LE MOUTON
FRENCH WAYS OF COOKING LAMB AND MUTTON

Generally speaking lamb and mutton recipes are interchangeable. Both have their devotees and arguments abound about whether to eat either underdone. A lot of people argue that mutton should be eaten well-hung and cooked pink, while lamb is best if hung less and cooked more. I like my lamb and mutton juicy and pink inside but I don't want to get into a fight about it. Mutton is better for stews because it has a fuller flavour. Cheaper cuts are most flavourful. For a stew many cooks like to blend *poitrine* and *collet*.

NECK. Gelatinous, good for stews.

BREAST. Can be slowly roasted if all fat trimmed. Excellent for braises or stewing.

SHOULDER. Bone, roll and braise or roast. Serve with chestnut garnish or beans. Good for *blanquettes*, fricassée or stew.

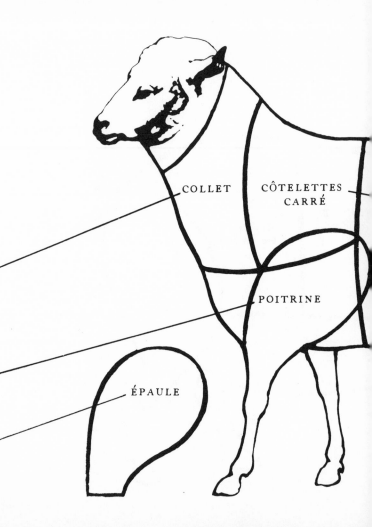

COLLET

CÔTELETTES CARRÉ

POITRINE

ÉPAULE

40

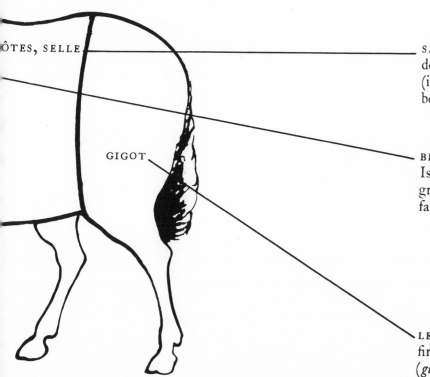

CÔTES, SELLE

GIGOT

SADDLE. Loin chops (*côtes*) are from here. Saddle is double-width joint of loin; it can be roasted or braised (if you have a pot big enough). Loin joints are often boned and rolled.

BEST END OF NECK AND MIDDLE NECK (U.S. RIB). Is usually cut into cutlets in France and then sautéed, grilled or braised. It can be a joint though if you trim fat and remove chine bone. Roast it about 45 mins.

LEG. Can be roasted as it is, or boned and marinaded first. Mutton leg can be braised or poached in water (*gigot à l'anglaise*) and served with onion sauce.

LES FROMAGES

The simplest way to categorize cheese is into fresh (home-made cream cheese), fermented (Brie and Camembert) and cooked (Port du Salut and Gruyère). But the process of cheese-making is so complex that even the U.S. Department of Agriculture admits there is no satisfactory way to classify cheeses. Certainly the soft unripened cheeses (Petit-Suisse, Boursin or the very creamy Fontainebleu) are a distinct group, but ripening such soft cheese by cultivating bacteria and mould-yeasts on the surface of the cheese to form a skin transforms them into the very sophisticated Brie and Camembert upon which France's reputation for cheese-making largely depends.

The law about cheese names varies from country to country, and in Germany a Camembert might well be locally made, as it is in the U.S.A. However, in France it is still possible to get the real thing. There you will find that a Brie de Coulommiers – fresh and mild – is different to a Brie de Melun – long cured and therefore stronger in taste – while Brie de Meaux is riper and has a different texture too. It is the best one in my opinion. Watch for *fermier* on the label to show it is farm-made: *laitier* means it's mass-produced.

When we first came to live in the country, milk from our neighbour's cow gave us a chance to try making our own 'camembert'. It was difficult and time-consuming but the result was excellent (although I was the only one who dared eat it). But I never did try to convert the same soft cheese into one of the blue cheeses that are ripened by interior mould. Roquefort is a famous example and a genuine one gets its distinctive flavour from the use of ewe's milk, rather than cow's milk which goes into Bleu d'Auvergne and every other French blue cheese. Stilton remains the supreme example of such blue cheeses providing it is soft, moist and well-matured. Bresse Bleu is not one of the best French cheeses.

These blue cheeses are usually classified as semi-soft cheeses (compared to the soft Brie etc.). Also in the semi-soft group are those ripened by surface micro-organisms as well as bacteria. Port du Salut is such a cheese.

Hard cheeses also come in two distinct types. Easily recognized by the holes that the processing makes are Emmenthal and Gruyère, whereas the Cheddar types have no holes. This group of cheeses is the broad basis of the cheese trade. Thousands of rubbery imitations abound throughout the world. These are the cheeses of the sandwich trade and the quick-lunch counter. The real thing will be rare and expensive but it is worth seeking.

A young Parmesan cheese (three months) is a delicious table cheese and would be included in the semi-soft category. But these *grana* cheeses are more usually cured to a state of hardness so that they are suitable for grating. In either case this is a luxury cheese and the price of genuine Parmesan – more accurately called Parmigiano-Reggiano – confirms this beyond doubt. Just as France is known as the home of the finest soft cheeses, so Italy has virtually monopolized the manufacture of very hard cheeses.

The quality and condition of cheese is of paramount importance. Far better serve one fine piece than a large variety of less than perfect pieces. In France cheese is invariably served before the dessert, while bread and wine are still on the table. Red wine is usually preferred with cheese, although the less serious fresh cheeses are sometimes accompanied by medium sweet white wines or a *rosé*.

Processed cheese is made by heating and emulsifying great vats of cheese mixtures. The result is not cheese in the best sense of the word, although it is sometimes quite nourishing. Such items are widely eaten in France and are very often dressed up in elaborate garnishes, such as walnuts or grapes, and attractive wrappings. These can often cost more than an equal quantity of real cheese. Rather than any of these flavoured concoctions, serve the very simple Fromage Blanc Frais, a fresh cheese from France widely available in England. This is ideally eaten with a dab of cream and a dusting of fine sugar.

In cooking, cheese is one of the most versatile foods. Grilled Gruyère on onion soup (in France simply called a *gratinée*) becomes a stringy tangle, while Parmesan sprinkled on minestrone makes a quite different soft crust. The low melting point of certain cheeses can provide a 'sauce' for such snacks as the *croque-monsieur* (a type of hot fried sandwich with ham). Cheese combines particularly well with veal and chicken, and vegetables such as potato, leeks, fennel, spinach, cauliflower and broccoli.

LES CORPS GRAS

In Southern France olive oil is the favourite – Provence oil for preference. Central and S.W. France and also Alsace use a lot of goose fat. In the North butter is the prevailing flavour. Nowadays, due to cost and health claims, the tasteless vegetable oils are found all over France.

OLIVE OIL. Buy the very best oil you can afford and buy it by the gallon – the tiny bottles are unreasonably priced. Wine merchants often stock the finest oil. *Vierge Extra* is the usual mark of oil obtained from the preliminary pressing. It is well worth the high price but reserve it for salads, cold dishes and cooking lightly flavoured foods.

BUTTER. The sediment causes it to burn very easily. (To clarify, see page 118.) A little oil added to butter will raise the temperature at which it will burn. This is the finest fat for flavour, and foods cooked in it go golden brown.

VEGETABLE OILS are made from maize, peanuts, seeds, etc. Usually they have no taste whatsoever and they are sometimes mixed with olive oil to modify the flavour (not in my house, they're not).

LARD. The finest – *lard gras* – is from the fat of the loin of the pig. It's in two layers; that nearest the skin is the firmest and so it's used for making *bardes* which are sheets of fat for protecting the outside of roast meat and chicken. It is also cut into strips, called *lardons*, that are stitched through meat that would otherwise be dry (more about this on pages 186–7). The layer underneath is easier to melt and is used for cooking. It is particularly popular in S.W. France. This rendered-down pork fat is called *saindoux*; it's what you get inside a packet marked Lard in Britain or the U.S.A. *Saindoux* is fine for pastry making. Other parts of a pig, e.g. the head and the belly, make fine fat. The latter is called *lard maigre*.

There are other types of lard, stuff rather like bacon called *lard fumé*, and salt pork fat – *lard salé* – which can be from loin or belly and is a popular flavouring for stews and hot-pots.

DRIPPING. Fat from roast pork or beef will often settle with a layer of rich brown jellied gravy at the bottom. The fat of beef and pork is best kept separate and used within a couple of days. Mutton fat is not normally used. Brisket slow-roasted gives first-rate dripping, so does pig's head and pig's belly.

LAMB KIDNEY FAT is a special item. A little of it rendered can be used to fry items that will benefit from its flavour, e.g. a mixed grill.

CHICKEN FAT. Nowadays sold separately and cheaply by many shops. Fine delicate flavour but don't use it in anything where solidifying is important – i.e. a *terrine* – because it keeps its soft semi-liquid texture. (Goose fat is superb but too scarce here for regular use.)

BEEF SUET. The only real stuff is that bought in a piece and grated at home (my Kenwood grating attachment simplifies this). Use it in pastry, pudding making and deep-frying.

MARROW. Obtained from inside pieces of marrowbone. A favourite method is to take two-inch lengths of marrowbone (butcher will slice them) and poach for about twenty minutes, then carefully remove the soft marrow. Spread on toast, this is served with *pot-au-feu*. It also makes a good garnish for vegetables instead of butter.

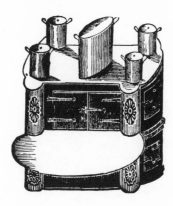

LA CARTE DES VINS,
CHAMPAGNE ET AUTRES ALCOOLS

MIS EN BOUTEILLE AU CHÂTEAU

CHATEAU LAFITE - ROTHSCHILD
1928

There are no rules about what wine to drink with what except the dictates of your palate. Experts merely suggest what will prove nasty. Snobs have built these suggestions into a cult that makes the Japanese Tea Ceremony look like beer drunk from a can. Here are simple rules. You can commit them to memory in five minutes:

There are four basic types of table wine –

1. White⎫
2. Red ⎬ Bordeaux
　　　　　

3. White⎫
4. Red ⎬ Burgundy

1. White ⎱ Bordeaux 3. White ⎱ Burgundy
2. Red ⎰   4. Red ⎰

If you know the character of these four you can decide what to order in a restaurant or what to serve to your guests, for almost all other wines fall into these same groups. Your wine waiter will know what you want if you name one of these groups and ask him what other (e.g. Italian) wine will correspond to the group of your choice. Don't be afraid of consulting the wine waiter – he will be flattered; ask him what is good value and he will respond.

WHITE BORDEAUX

1. Bordeaux wines come in bottles this shape so you can recognize the group even before you spot the label. The bottle was designed like this to trap the sediment while the wine is poured.

There are some rather dry white Bordeaux wines – notably the dry Graves – but for the most part these whites are inclined to range from mellow to very sweet. Some experts like those not too sweet white wines served with *foie gras* or perhaps a sole in rich sauce; some say the finest accompaniment for a fish *pâté* is a chilled white Sauterne which is very sweet. O.K.; that's what they say but if you take my advice you'll leave experiments like that for someone else's liver. Drink these white Bordeaux wines cold with the sweet course when they will taste fresh and sharp because they contrast with the greater sweetness of the dessert.

RED BORDEAUX

2. Red wines are usually drier than white wines because they include the skin in the manufacture and the skin of a grape has a rather bitter taste – try it. Red wines from the Bordeaux region are called clarets, they are lighter and thinner in body than the Burgundy reds that I'll mention in a moment. Red Bordeaux is the wine to be served with any meaty dish, but because it is light in weight it goes especially well with the delicate meats. Serve it with veal, pork, lamb, goose, or duck. It's also great with a *pasta* and meat sauce or with fried chicken. This is the backbone of your cellar.

Half-way Reds

There are exceptions in the ranks of the Red Bordeaux: there are a few districts where the wine is heavier and full-bodied to the point of resembling a Red Burgundy (see under). The St Émilion and the Pomerol are wines that can replace a Red Burgundy. Have some in the cellar, taste them and compare them with the other red wines there.

WHITE BURGUNDY

3. Now come the other great pair of wine types – the Burgundies. The bottle is always this shape.

The White Burgundies are a really exclusive group of wines; unlike the other three in my simplified list these are the inimitable ones. They are never very cheap, they are flavourful, and very, very dry. They can go anywhere and accompany anything that is edible. These great wines are best reserved to accompany food that needs a fine astringent flavour. Serve them with the shellfish, lobster, oysters, crab, or when you feel a touch of chilled extravagance suits the mood.

RED BURGUNDY

4. Red Burgundy is a mixed group of wines. The finest Red Burgundies are matchless and of incredible price. The simpler ones (e.g. Beaujolais) are everyday affairs. The more expensive it is the more it will have 'Red Burgundy' character. The cheaper ones will be lighter and thinner and can be treated almost like Red Bordeaux. So if you have a fine quality Red Burgundy (and I strongly advise that a half-bottle of the real thing is worth half a gallon of the mixed-up blended stuff) it should be drunk with the powerful types of food. Serve it with roast beef and those stews and braises that have been marinaded. Serve it with a fine piece of steak, kidneys, or a well-hung item of game. Some of those light meats that I said would be good with Red Bordeaux might be better with Red Burgundy if the sauce in which they are served is dark and highly flavoured. A good Red Burgundy is sometimes so fine that you want the food to be merely a background to the wine. For this reason simple buttered *pasta* or any cheese is a wonderful partner for good Red Burgundy.

Here is a simple wine-cellar:

NO. BOTS.	LABEL SAYS	IDEAL DRINKING TEMP. ° F.	TYPE	USE IT WITH
12	Médoc	64+	Red Bordeaux	Light meats, poultry, etc. This is the backbone of your cellar.
4	Sauternes	50	White Bordeaux	Dessert, fruit. Sweet wine, not suitable for savoury course.
8	Dry Graves	52	White Bordeaux	The driest one of its type. O.K. with white fish etc. Compare with White Burgundy.
3	Chambertin	60	Red Burgundy	Fine robust red for game, steak or a super stew. Expensive.
4	St Émilion	64+	Red Bordeaux (but heavier than usual)	Half-way between Red Burgundy and Red Bordeaux. Wonderful with steak or a lighter type of stew.
4	Beaujolais	60	Red Burgundy (but lighter than usual)	Use it like the St Émilion; it's another half-way wine. Can be served cold.
3	Pouilly Fuissé	52	White Burgundy	Luxury shell-fish.

A really good wine merchant will store your wines in his cellar for a very small charge indeed. You collect them as you want them. He will advise you what to buy according to how many years ahead you plan to drink them. The proportions of the types are my suggestions; your wine merchant may have other ideas – so might you!

If you decide to store them yourself, choose a quiet place that is about 55° F. (if it's above 65° F. it's not suitable). The temperature must be steady, so it's no good using a draughty passage. The bottles should be out of the light, and that includes electric light or even candlelight. There must be no vibration there and letting your guests maul them around won't help.

When you serve the wine, red wine should be uncorked and allowed to come to the temperature of an ordinary living-room. Ideally put it in the living-room 48 hours before; don't warm it artificially. White wines and *rosés* are served chilled. Sweet white wines are colder still. Decanting is not necessary unless you want to show off your decanter. A good large wine glass (restaurant style) is suitable for serving any wine including champagne.

ROSÉ WINE. Too often chosen as a compromise between red and white, it is nothing of the sort. Drink it with cold food – aspics, etc., or on a hot day.

SPARKLING WINES. There are many of them (e.g. sparkling Hock), including Champagne. Follow the notes I have given for white wines. Treat dry Champagne like dry white wine, sweet Champagne like sweet white wine.

COGNAC. There is an old saying that a poor earth yields a good grape, that a good grape yields a poor wine but a poor wine produces a superb brandy. Certainly Folle-Blanche, from which Cognac is made, is very awful-tasting stuff. When a Frenchman wants a glass of brandy, he is likely to order a *'fine'*; he receives a glass of brandy made in the great brandy-producing area called La Grande Champagne which includes the towns of Segonzac, Jarnac, and of course Cognac.

The 'suburbs' of La Grande Champagne are called La Petite Champagne and to the north is the third-best brandy area – Les Borderies. Surrounding the whole area is Les Bois which also produces brandy. All these brandies are called Cognac.

ARMAGNAC. This is another brandy highly regarded by experts. The finest Armagnac is without doubt better than second-best Cognac. The best comes from a region called Le Bas-Armagnac.

CALVADOS is a substantially different drink; it is a spirit based upon distilled cider and for this reason is mostly found in Brittany and Normandy. The taste is strongly apple-like and rather refreshing. Although brandy is always served at room temperature, Calvados is excellent served with ice.

EAU DE VIE OR MARC. Marc is the pips and skins left from the wine-making press. This pulp is distilled into a powerful juice usually called either Eau de vie or Marc and available in almost every farmhouse in France. Marc de Bourgogne is particularly good. It is usually almost colourless. Variants of this distillation are found wherever wine is pressed. In Italy it is Grappa. There's something of pot luck in choosing them, but a good one is tremendous.

BRANDIES of any sort should be served in a largish glass, preferably one that has a small top (so that the aroma is liberated but doesn't float away). A warm hand around the brandy will bring it to just the right temperature – ain't nature wonderful? However, a customer ordering a *fine* in a French café gets it usually in a tiny glass brim-full.

Brandy does not 'age' in bottles but only in casks. Many experts believe that England's climate is a fine one in which to 'age' brandies and for that reason will give top marks to a brandy stored (in casks) in England. Many of the very fine brandies are used to bolster mediocre ones and the great brandies are becoming scarcer and more expensive. There's no reason why you shouldn't get your wine merchant to buy and store a cask (it can be a tiny one) for you, but you will have to wait a long time for it to come to maturity. In France a cask is sometimes given as a christening or wedding present.

Oddly enough brandy doesn't get stronger and stronger the older it gets, and in any case the expert often prefers a light one. Colour is usually added and is not a good sign; watch out also for the taste of vanilla which seems to be on the increase. Tax does not increase with the value of the brandy and you therefore get a slightly better deal if you buy one of the very expensive 'vintage' labels.

CHAMPAGNE

It's not difficult to make Champagne that will sell at far below the price that is charged for the best. For instance you could use second-hand bottles instead of using new ones or, as is very common nowadays, use crown corks for the early stages or second quality corks. Instead of adding Cognac to it you could add neutral spirit. You could own land with vines so that you could have a regular supply instead of bidding for the best grapes. You could use tanks instead of casks which have to be checked and looked after. Even more of a saving would be effected by buying the third pressing from a company who have already taken the first two for themselves.

Another way of saving money is not to use the 'Champagne Method' at all. Instead of its happening in the bottle in which it is sold, the process takes place within large tanks and the bottling comes afterwards. Even more money can be saved by just cooling wine off and forcing low pressure carbon dioxide into it. Tank-made sparkling wines are sometimes marked *'Cuve Clos'* and those forced with gas are marked *'Vins Mousseux'*.

As you see, the process is a very complex one. The temperature at which the champagne is kept is very important and at one stage the cellars are opened and the cold air causes a precipitation which throws off the impurities. A later sediment is more of a problem and over a long period the bottles are stored with the neck very low so that the sediment drops towards the cork. The cellarman taps the bottles with lessening degrees of agitation so that the sediment slides towards the cork. This process alone can take three months. Eventually the neck of the bottle is frozen so that the sediment is imprisoned in a small block of ice. The bottle is opened at this stage and the ice flies out with a bang. The bottle is topped up, tested for flaws, and the contents checked, and a sweetener is added if it's to be sweet champagne. This may be five or six years later than the grape harvest and the champagne is still being made and given space by the manufacturer. Now a new cork is put in and wired down and the bottle is almost ready to be shipped; but there will probably be another two periods of resting (at least six months each).

I have gone into all this detail to make the point that Champagne is expensive with good reason. If you are going to drink Champagne there is a good argument for drinking a very good one. Bollinger, Veuve Clicquot, Heidsieck, Krug, Moët et Chandon, Mumm, are all old firms with excellent reputations, and each has its band of supporters.

When ordering remember that *brut* means Champagne as it comes: unsweetened. Champagne marked dry will be sweeter than *brut* and the semi-dry will be sweeter still. The one marked *sweet* is very sweet. There was a time when Frenchmen drank only sweet champagne and served it towards the end of the meal. Nowadays French taste follows the English style of dry champagne served early.

A *bottle* of Champagne holds 26 fluid ounces. If you will be drinking more than this a *magnum* holds twice as much, or for one person an *imperial pint* is just right. Champagne is also sold in half and quarter bottles but these will probably have been rebottled and are not the ones the Champagne has lived in for many years while being manufactured. A *jeroboam* holds four bottles and is the largest size normally used by humans. Champagne can be vintage (in which case the year will be marked on the label) or non-vintage. The latter from a good label is much better than a vintage Champagne from an inferior manufacturer. A vintage Champagne is usually drunk between 8 and 15 years after its vintage date. Champagne over 20 years old is a curiosity rather than a drink.

OTHER SPARKLING WINES. Bear in mind the definitions 'Méthode Champenoise', and 'Cuve Clos' and 'Vins Mousseux' mentioned above. The last two will be inferior and probably will lose their sparkle soon after being poured. Among the finest sparkling wines (after Champagne of course) are the Loire wines (Sparkling Vouvray and Sparkling Muscatel) and the Sparkling Burgundies (White, Pink, and Red are all well worth trying). From Germany there are Sparkling Hocks and Moselles, some of which are made by the true Champagne method.

THE APÉRITIF. Drink it while you read the menu, to sharpen the appetite. Most Frenchmen would choose a dry Vermouth. That's a combination of wine with brandy and herbs and spices. It's good advice to avoid the tougher alcohols – vodka mixes, gin, or whisky – when you are hungry, because it's then that the stomach is at its most vulnerable. Choose a Byrrh, a Lillet, or a Suze; they are gentle in action and natural in effect. A Dubonnet is too sweet to my taste before starting a meal unless you want to hamper your appetite. Perhaps a glass of dry white wine, nicely chilled, is the finest *apéritif* of all.

MINERAL WATERS. Perrier is the best-known one

perhaps because it's fizzy – *renforcée avec son propre gaz naturel* – but there are plenty of flat ones too. Evian is good for mixing, Vichy is slightly salt and Contrexéville has a reputation as a hang-over cure. Mineral water is something I order frequently; it provides a glass of something to toy with when you face an afternoon of hard work. It's a suitable accompaniment to hot foods or foods that you are particularly interested in, e.g. trying to guess what the cook put into it. It's the drink the driver drinks when I'm the passenger. Malvern Water is an excellent home-grown product.

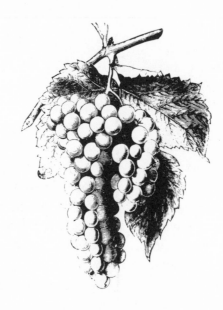

LA CUISINE FRANÇAISE ET LE FROID

Nothing that comes out of a deep freezer is going to taste better than it was before it went in. However, in the hands of a clever cook the freezer can be a useful tool. There are three basic, and very different, ways of using a freezer. Its prime use is for country people who put away half a pig or a fieldful of broccoli and use it piecemeal. The second type of user is the one who lives a long way away from the stores and wants to shop once a week or even less. Thirdly there is the cook like us who is prepared to go to the trouble of making savarins, pizzas, cassoulets, and braises but who wants to make such things in bulk (which is no more trouble) and use them as wanted.

The first two types of user need no advice from me but the third might find these notes interesting and useful.

VEGETABLES

table on pages 67–8

Make your choice and:

1. Sort and briefly rinse. Cut them into pieces if you like.
2. Blanch in fast-boiling water (page 194).
3. Refresh (page 194) in ice-cold water.

4. Drain well and dry them.
5. Wrap them. Put them into polythene bags or into those soft plastic boxes sold for refrigerator storage. The more air-tight the container is, the better. The less air there is inside the pack, the better. Bags are useful in this respect because they can be squeezed to fit the shape of the food.
6. Mark container with a label or with a wax pencil showing the date and the type of food and the amount (e.g. 4 portions of beans).
7. Place in the coolest part of the freezer (most freezers have a freezing platform). After 24 hours stack with other frozen food.

FRUIT

table on page 66

The easiest way to handle it is to make a *compote*, i.e. poach it in syrup. An easy syrup is a 40 per cent syrup. That's 4 cups of hot water with 3 cups of sugar stirred into it. Cook the fruit till it's almost the way you want to eat it, then let it cool down before freezing it. Since you'll probably only want to do this with the choicest part of the fruit the off-cuts can be made into a fruit purée which can also be frozen.

Some fruits are O.K. without any syrup on them, e.g. all kinds of currants and raspberries, and also rhubarb. Another way of handling almost any fruit is to put a layer of sugar – not much – over each layer of fruit, finishing with the sugar. Whenever possible add a little lemon juice, for this will preserve colour and flavour. The amount is the juice of one large lemon to one and a half pints of water or its equivalent. A more scientific approach to preserving colour and flavour is to add half a teaspoon of crystalline ascorbic acid to every one and a half pints of liquid, but it's not available everywhere; have a word with your chemist if you intend to deep-freeze fruit for long periods. For short periods the sugar will be good enough.

MEAT, POULTRY, FISH

Meat, poultry or fish can also be frozen. Clean and trim. Divide into sections as if preparing for cooking. Wrap in foil or a polythene bag, excluding air as much as you can. Try to avoid pockets of air inside the food (e.g. stuffed poultry is not a good thing to deep-freeze for that reason). Mark and put it in the coldest part of the freezer with plenty of air around it until it's quite frozen, then it can be stacked against other frozen food. Allow about 24 hours for a piece of food to freeze hard enough to be stacked. Date everything and use it in rotation. Every six months I clear my freezer, completely using everything. Then I defrost it, clean it and begin again with commercially frozen food, gradually replacing it with my own. Make sure that the commercially frozen food you put in your freezer has not been allowed partially to thaw by the shopkeeper. Many shops don't supervise the freezer cabinets closely enough, thinking that all their customers are going to use their purchases immediately. Be very critical of the place from which you buy frozen food; make sure you get it in good condition. Because this business of keeping frozen food very cold is so important you should never refreeze any item that has thawed. Your best plan is to store food in the size container you need. For example, if there are only two of you, don't freeze a gallon of rhubarb in one container; separate it into half-pint portions.

Now I come to the real reason for including this chapter on freezers in a book of French Cooking. The freezer can be used to store prepared foods (cooked and uncooked). Various pies can be wrapped in foil and frozen uncooked. Stocks and soups can be prepared in bulk and served weeks later. Uncooked pie shells can be stored for a couple of months. *Gnocchi, mousse, crêpes,* stew, *daubes,* braises, and *bavaroise* can be all ready in the freezer and served at short notice. It's an especially attractive idea because it is so little extra trouble to produce a greater bulk of a complex recipe. The basic rules for freezing are to freeze as rapidly as possible (i.e. don't crowd newly positioned things), label clearly, use foods in rotation; and finally, don't abuse the system by leaving food in there indefinitely.

Here are some more ideas from my notebook. N.B. All cooked foods that are to be served hot must be underdone because the warming-up will cook them a little.

1. STEW. Any sort is very good. Beef, mutton, etc.

2. PIES. Very good in a freezer but use lots of fat in making the pastry and make it butter or lard rather than one of the brand-name fats. Chicken, veal, beef, and steak and kidney are fine but pork loses flavour, so needs a little extra herbs or seasoning. If it's a pork pie using hot-water pastry it's best to cook it before freezing; short-pastry pies can be frozen raw or with raw pastry and cooked filling.

3. FRIED FISH is passable. Do it in egg and crumbs, warm it in oven after thawing it.

POACHED FISH is best frozen under a simple flour-type sauce, e.g. a cheese sauce.

4. WHOLE RAW CHICKEN. Best to buy a commercially frozen one. If you want to do it yourself don't have stuffing inside when you freeze it.

5. CHICKEN STEWS, FRICASSÉES AND CURRIES are excellent and use far less space than a whole chicken. For fricassée don't add the egg until it's thawed out.

6. FRIED CHICKEN takes too long to thaw out to be worth-while, and like fish is never really crisp.

7. TERRINE. Fine, but make sure that it has no jelly or air-pockets at the bottom of the dish.

8. SPONGE. Quite a useful thing to have tucked away. Ones with fat in are better than fat-free sort.

9. BREAD. Yeast lasts at least 6 months. Anything made with yeast can be frozen uncooked for about 6 weeks. I don't think that is worth-while. A better idea is to make a lot of bread and keep it in the freezer until you're ready to use it. Let it thaw right out before attempting to slice it.

10. POTATO. Mashed potato freezes quite well, so does the potato *galette* (page 202).

11. PASTA. Not worth it. But a really fine meat or tomato sauce made with chicken stock is worth freezing. It can be heated in a saucepan while the *pasta* is cooking.

12. SOUPS. Keep them simple, don't have creamy floury ones. Simple meat stock is probably best, but tomato, celery, mushroom or chicken type soups that can have cream added when they are thawed are useful.

13. EGGS, CREAM, OR SAUCES MADE FROM EGGS AND CREAM. Don't; only Cornish cream is O.K. and that's because it's been heat-treated. Even ice-cream won't keep very well.

14. BUTTER. Unsalted butter will keep for ages – as much as twelve months; salted less than half this time.

15. RAW MEAT. Not finely chopped meat, because it's got tiny air-pockets in it, but most meat is O.K. if you trim away the fat.

16. FISH. Clean it, trim it, wipe it clean.

17. CRAB, LOBSTER, SHRIMP, AND PRAWN. They all suffer quite badly. If you must do it, take the edible meat and put it under a flour-base sauce.

18. OYSTERS. Better than you'd imagine. Best way: remove from shells and pack in their own juice.

19. MEAT OR FISH, WRAPPED IN CABBAGE LEAVES OR INSIDE PIMENTO. These types of food will heat up well. If they are submerged in sauce or stock they are better cooked before freezing – cook them until almost done because the warming up will complete the action; if they are not in sauce, freeze them raw.

Learn from the way that frozen foods are packed and what foods the commercial companies choose to prepare. Remember, however, that a lot of commercial frozen food will not be stored for a long time and that frozen food plants have special equipment that freezes food to very low temperatures quickly.

(More prepared dishes pages 66–7)

FRUIT	TREATMENT
Apricots	1 min. in hot syrup. Cool syrup and fruit separately.
Berries (all kinds)	1 min. in hot syrup. Cool syrup and fruit separately.
Cherries	As above but less than 1 min.
Melons in slices or chunks	Cover with cold syrup.
Peaches, plums	Into cold syrup, but make sure they are quite ripe.
Rhubarb	For best results, chop and give 1 min. in hot syrup.
Strawberries	If ripe, into cold syrup.
Raspberries	Separate them (e.g. on a tray) until they are hard, then pack them into bags or boxes. This is the way commercial firms prepare peas.

PREPARED DISHES	PREFERABLY USE WITHIN	BUT WILL BE O.K. FOR	REMARKS
Braised meat, *Daube* etc.*	3 months	5 months	Thawing at warm room temp. is best but it can be heated with care.
Pastry shell (cooked)	2 months	2 months	
Pastry shell (uncooked)	2 months	3 months	
Gratin	2 months	3 months	Potato in it may go soggy.
Home made ice-cream, *Bavaroise*, *Charlotte Russe*	1 month	6 weeks	
Pancakes	2 months	10 weeks	Wax paper between each one. Tin foil around whole lot.
Soups, sauces	5 months	7 months	Line a bowl with tin foil, fill with soup. When frozen remove from bowl, wrap foil around.
Shop ice-cream	2 weeks	3 weeks	
Cooked meat sliced (in gravy or not)	1 month	4 months	Also applies to stews; beef curry is especially good.
Chicken pieces fried, grilled, or poached	1 month	3 months	

Cassoulet: for perfect results keep cooked beans separate. Heat, combine, then serve.

VEGETABLES	BLANCHING TIME	REMARKS
Green beans, etc.	3 mins	
Broccoli	3 mins	For best results have flowerlets all the same size.
Corn on the cob	10 mins	Don't crowd them when freezing.
Whole kernel corn	Cook whole cobs 4 mins	Scrape kernels off cobs when they are drained. This is much more economical for space.
Mushroom, sliced or small	none	Fry very lightly. Cool.
Peas	$1\frac{1}{2}$ mins	
Pimentos	3 mins	Split in half and remove seeds before blanching them. N.B. If not blanched, the wrapped raw pimentos will last a month.
Carrots	Whole tiny, 5 mins, diced, 2 mins	

LE LEXIQUE ET LE MENU

Agneau. Lamb. 5–9 months. (*Mouton* is mutton between one and two years old.)

Agneau de lait. Milk-fed lamb, 2 or 3 months old.

Agneau de pré-salé. Lamb from the salty northern grasslands called *les prés-salés*. (Just as Bresse after a chicken shows that it comes from Bresse – a good place for chickens.)

Aigo Bouido. A Mediterranean garlic soup.

Aiguillette. Top of the rump, a small, very lean braising joint of beef. On menus it's called *pièce de bœuf* (which see).

Ail. Garlic.

Aioli. Powerful garlic mayonnaise which is used on hot or cold boiled fish, stirred into fish soup or melted over green vegetables and boiled potatoes.

Aloyau. Sirloin.

Andouillettes. Small sausages made from chitterlings (intestines, tripe) normally bought ready-made, grilled, and served hot.

Arroser. To baste.

Aspic. A finished cold dish involving jelly (*gelée*).

Baba au rhum. See *savarin*.

Bain-marie. Originally a deep water-filled recess in a solid-fuel stove. Pans of sauce kept here were warm enough to serve but not hot enough to continue cooking (and so spoil). Nowadays a *bain-marie* is a heavy metal water-jacket with handles and specially designed lidded pans that fit inside. It is filled with warm water and stands on the stove-top. The instruction 'cook *au bain-marie*' should not be taken too literally; it means cook at a low temperature. See *étuvée* and *poêle, à la*.

Bard. Using thin sheets of pork fat (*bardes de lard*) to protect (e.g. breast of a roasting chicken).

Bardes de lard. Thin sheets of pork fat usually cut from under skin of loin (*lard gras*). Apart from barding it's used to line a *terrine*.

Béchamel. Nowadays always a very simple white sauce. See page 126.

Beekenohfe. A thick hot-pot from Alsace very like

Lancashire hot-pot. It consists of layers of potato, onion, mutton, and pork moistened with dry white wine and cooked either *étuvée* or in a double-boiler.

Beurre noir. Butter heated to a dark brown (not black) colour. Used hot to garnish fish or brains.

Beurres composés. Flavoured butters (cold) used for garnishing hot dishes, for basting, stirring into soup or for décor. To make it, cream butter well, then beat in chosen flavouring (mashed), a teaspoon at a time. Flavourings: crushed garlic, mustard, anchovy, egg yolks, lemon juice, chopped herbs, onion juice.

Bifteck. A very vague term meaning some sort of steak.

Bifteck haché. A hamburger. See page 190.

Bigarade. Dressing made from peel and juice of bitter oranges.

Bind. To make a mixture 'glue' together; become thicker.

Blanch (Fr. *blanchir*). Cook in boiling water, sometimes for a very short period as when skinning tomatoes or almonds.

Blend. Mix very well. Nowadays this may mean in a food-blending machine: a glass heat-proof goblet containing small whirling blades.

Blind. Of pastry case, cooked empty.

Bœuf au gros sel. See *gros sel*.

Bœuf salé. Salt beef (usually brisket) that's been in brine. Don't confuse with *bœuf au gros sel*.

Bonne femme. Simply cooked (housewife style). Often includes potato.

Boudin. 'Black pudding', a sausage made from pork blood.

Bouillabaisse. A fish stew made from at least six different types of sea-fish and shellfish too. Originates on Mediterranean coast between Toulon and Marseilles. In Marseilles it will probably have lobster and eel added to it, nearer to Toulon perhaps just one tiny crab. In Paris it's served with mussels and oysters. The other ingredients are a generous amount of olive oil and garlic, saffron, tomato, onion, fennel, parsley, and bay leaf. Technically interesting because it's the only flesh food dish that's boiled furiously (this causes the oil and water in which it's cooked to emulsify) and must be done without letting the fish pieces break up. Unlike *matelote* (*q.v.*) a *bouillabaisse* never has wine in it.

Bouilli. Boiled beef, the meat from the *pot-au-feu – bœuf bouilli*.

Bouillie. Milk, sugar, and starch (flour or rice-flour, etc.) into which egg yolks and butter are whipped. The result is a little like *crème pâtissière* and together with *béchamel* it forms one of the three (very similar) ways to begin a *soufflé*.

Bouillir. A big, roaring boiling-up. A more gentle boil is called *mijoter*, in which case it just bubbles now and again at the same place. (See also *frémir*.)

Bouillon. Clear meat stock. See *consommé*, page 132.

Boulangère. This is a dish which you took to the baker's shop and cooked in his oven so it usually means long, slow cooking.

Bouquet garni. A group of herbs: parsley, thyme, bay, etc.

Braise. To cook covered (in a *braisière* originally) at a heat above the boiling point of water. Small amounts of stock poured over the food form a moist film. All-around heat is needed, so it can't be cooked on a stove-top. Compare *daube*, *étuvée*, and stew.

Bresse. A part of France where the finest poultry are raised – it doesn't indicate a way of cooking.

Brochet. Pike. *Quenelles de brochet* are soft 'dumplings' of pike.

Brut. Dry (lit. crude or raw). Describes the driest type of champagne and indicates that no sweet syrup has been added.

Caramelize. Heat sugar till it goes light brown.

Cassoulet. A thick hot-pot type of dish made from goose, pork, and beans.

Cervelas. A smoked sausage.

Chair à saucisse. Sausage meat sold in French butchers' shops. There is no satisfactory English equivalent unless you make it.

Chantilly. Whipped cream usually with a trace of sugar and vanilla. French cream is slightly fermented and therefore thicker than its English equivalent.

Châteaubriant. A prime cut of beef, originally (and sometimes still) a piece of steak in which the *contre-filet* is still attached to the *filet*. (Like a porterhouse with the bone removed.) Since in French butchery nowadays the *filet* is removed from the *contre-filet* at an early stage, they usually serve you a very thick slice of *filet* instead. A real Châteaubriant can weigh up to $1\frac{3}{4}$ lb., a double-thick *filet* about $\frac{1}{2}$ lb. See also page 188.

Compote. Fruit (fresh or dried) cooked in syrup.

Confit d'oie. Goose cooked and then preserved in its own fat. Usually a goose that has been raised to make *foie gras* from its liver.

Contre-filet. See *faux-filet*.

Couenne. Thick pork skin. Highly regarded as a flavouring ingredient for French braises, stews, and soups. Ask your butcher for some.

Coulis. Thick purée of meat or vegetables.

Crêpe. Pancake.

Crépinettes. Small, flat sausages wrapped in caul (*crépine*: membrane enclosing paunch) which imparts a delicious flavour. Such sausages are very easy to make and quite delicious if you have a sheet of *crépine*. English butchery trade throws it away.

Croquettes. Cakes made from cooked meat or fish. See page 162.

Croûtons. Tiny cubes of bread fried crisp. Used as a garnish, especially for thick soups.

Cube. To cut into small cubes.

Cuillère. Spoon; '*napper la cuillère*' means thick enough to coat a spoon.

Cure. Preserve by hanging in smoke, salting, or drying.

Darne. A slice of fish.

Daube. Marinaded meat – whole or cubed – cooked in a closed pot, originally in a *daubière*. (For fuller description see cookstrip page 186). The wet marinade prevents you frying the meat before cooking it, and this is the fundamental difference between *bœuf Bourguignon* (which is a *daube*) and a *coq au vin* (which is a *fricassée*).

Decant. Pour out, letting sediment remain.

Déglacer. Rinse out, e.g. meat juices from a pan using stock, wine or brandy. When alcohol is used it is boiled while being stirred.

Dégraisser. Degrease. To remove fat, e.g. from the top of hot liquids. See page 116.

Désosser. To remove bones, e.g. from a leg of lamb.

Dessert wine. Sweet, still wine containing about 20 per cent alcohol, e.g. Port, Sherry, Muscatel. But not Sauternes, no matter how sweet.

Dice. To cut into tiny cubes (*couper en dés*); this is one stage beyond *julienne*. See page 114.

Duxelles. A special mushroom paste.

Entrecôte. A prime beef cut from between the ribs, Wing Ribs in British butchery. A *contre-filet* is often served instead.

Épigramme. Lit. an invented item. Often slice of breast of lamb fried in egg and breadcrumbs.

Escalope (or collop). Thin slice of veal taken from the *noix*, $\frac{3}{8}$ in. thick flattened to less than $\frac{1}{4}$ in. by beating. Sometimes this word is used incorrectly in a vaguer sense.

Escargots. Snails; vineyard snail is the best. Usually cooked in garlic and butter and replaced in shell to serve.

Estouffade. 'A smothering'. To cook the food like that; tightly closed, i.e. in a *daubière*.

Étuvée. As braise but at a heat below the boiling point of water. Because of this the food will give off its own moisture and will need none added. Such cooking can be done in a double-boiler or in a very low oven. Generous butter is always used in this type of cooking.

Faux-filet. Same as *contre-filet*. It is the loin part of a sirloin, i.e. not the tenderloin (*filet*) part. It's a prime cut of beef.

Filet. A prime cut of beef. '*Le filet*' is the tenderloin (or undercut of fillet) of a steak – as against a *contre-filet*. ('*Un filet*' means a flat serving of meat or fish without bone.) See page 188.

Fillet. Either meaning of French word '*filet*'. Also means ribs or a leg cut.

Fines herbes. A selected mixture of herbs. In France it sometimes means almost entirely parsley.

Flambé. In flames, by igniting warmed alcohol, e.g. brandy.

Foie gras. Two sorts; goose liver and duck liver from Alsace and Toulouse, specially prepared by force feeding. If it says '*en bloc*' you will get a chunk of liver but if it says '*pâté foie gras*' you might get anything at all, for this means that there is some *foie gras* in there somewhere.

Fouetter. To beat with fork, spoon, wire-whisk, electric beater, or anything you like.

Four, au. Baked in oven.

Frangipane. A very stiff pastry cream (see *crème pâtissière*, page 146) with crushed almonds, macaroons, and sometimes Kirsch.

Frémir. To shiver; a description of the slight movement on the surface of the water when foods are poached (see also *bouillir*).

Fricandeau. Rump of veal. Also means cooked veal; loin braised or roasted.

Fricassée. Meat lightly fried, then stewed. On menu usually means white meat or poultry in egg and cream sauce.

Garbure. A hot-pot or soup of cabbage and beans.

Gigot. In France this word for leg always means a '*gigot entier*' which is the whole leg up to and including the tail. In France stuffed lamb implies that a leg will be served because the way the shoulder is cut doesn't make it suitable for stuffing.

Girofle. Clove.

Gras-double. The three stomachs of an ox, called in England tripe (the French word *tripes* is slightly different).

Gratin. A shallow dish, a brown covering or a cooked item, served in a *gratin* dish.

Gratin, au. To brown under the grill, usually a covering of crumbs and butter.

Gratiner. To brown – under the grill.

Gros sel. Sea salt, the finest type of salt. It's in large grains, so is often put inside a salt-mill on the table so that it can be crushed. *Bœuf au gros sel* is boiled beef (see *pot-au-feu*, page 130). It's served hot with vegetables and is sprinkled with sea salt. N.B. It is not salt beef.

Hacher. To chop very fine.

Haricot. Beans; white, brown, or green.

Haricot. A stew, probably from word *halicoter*, to cut up. N.B. A haricot doesn't contain haricot beans.

Incorporer. Fold. Blend together gently.

Jarret. Knuckle.

Julienne. Strips of vegetables. See page 114.

Jus. Gravy.

Lard. Piece of pork fat used for larding meat (see page 188). Also means dripping made by rendering pork fat (page 166), a particularly worthwhile item to have available.

Lard gras. A section of fresh pork fat taken from the skin of the loin. (N.B. French pigs have more fat here than English pigs have.) '*Bardes de lard*' – thin sheets of fat for protecting roasted items (e.g. chicken breast) – are made from *lard gras*.

Longe. Top end of loin (sirloin is from the word *surlonge*).

Macérer. As marinade but for fruit, made from the sugar and liquor, etc.

Maigre, au. For Lent, i.e. meatless, or a dish without garnish.

Mange-tout. Yellow waxy peas in pod. Called in Britain 'sugar peas'. The whole thing including the pod is eaten.

Marinade (Fr. *mariner*). To immerse in a liquid to tenderize and give flavour; meat usually goes into a marinade of oil, wine, vinegar, onion, garlic, bay, brandy. Or at least some of them.

Marinade cuite. Cooked marinade. The vegetables are lightly fried, alcohol is scalded. Use when cold.

Mariné. Pickled.

Marmite. A tall narrow saucepan which, due to shape, has a slow rate of evaporation.

Matelote. Fish stew made with pieces of freshwater fish, e.g. carp, perch, pike, etc., and any dry wine (red or white).

Médaillons. See *tournedos*.

Mélanger. To mix; but not to beat, which is fiercer.

Meunière, à la. Served in butter that has been cooked light brown (*noisette*).

Mignon (*filet*). A slice from the small, pointed end of the *filet* (*queue de filet*). It is therefore a small *filet*. This is the piece you see in most T-bone steaks.

Mignonnette. See *tournedos*. Also name for coarsely ground pepper.

Mimosa. Garnished with hard-boiled egg, chopped.

Mornay. A *béchamel* sauce with cheese.

Mousseline. Lots of things take this name as soon as they have whipped cream added. Small moulds of creamed, puréed meat, fish, or poultry for instance, or sauces like *hollandaise* and *mayonnaise* become *hollandaise mousseline* and *mayonnaise mousseline* after cream is added. Certain meats, forcemeats, and certain types of delicate pastry also take this name.

Nap (Fr. *napper*). To cover with a thick cream sauce. See also *cuillère*.

Noisettes. See *tournedos*.

Omble chevalier. Char – a very highly thought of, trout-like fish from Savoy region of France. Also lives in English and Welsh mountain lakes.

Paner. Coat with breadcrumbs.

Pannequets. Stuffed pancakes.

Papillote. Oiled paper case or envelope in which fish or meat is cooked. See page 170.

Parboil. Precook, as blanch. See page 116.

Parmentier. The introduction of the potato was a momentous event. Yield per acre was better than beet and the threat of famine considerably decreased. The Frenchman responsible for popularizing the potato has left his name to mark its presence on menus.

Pâte. Pastry, bread-dough or batter. Originally tarts were made with bread-dough.

Pâte brisée. Short pastry.

Pâte demi-feuilletée. Rerolled off-cuts from flaky pastry. Suited to hot pies, while the better flaky pastry is reserved for cold dishes.

Pâte feuilletée. Flaky pastry.

Pâté; Pâté en croûte. Meat or fish enclosed in pastry on all sides. Often pâté is used wrongly to describe a '*terrine*' (which see) but a very rich liver preparation of this sort is always called a *pâté*, crust or no crust. See *foie gras*.

Paupiette. A thin slice of meat wrapped around a stuffing then cooked – often braised.

Petit salé. Pork (belly or odd corners) salted in brine, not dry salted.

Pièce de bœuf. A description often seen on French menus. It means a large (6 lb.) cut of rump which is a prime beef cut. Instead of being served slightly underdone, as is usual with first-quality cuts of beef, it has long slow cooking. The butcher calls this same

cut of beef *pointe de culotte*.

Pipérade basquaise. A type of omelette from Béarn. To make it, chop up some flesh of tomato and sweet peppers and cook them until tender. The seeds are of course discarded. In France they might hold the peppers over a gas flame to remove the skin and this leaves the peppers with a fugitive scorched flavour that is often found in North African cooking. When the chopped pieces are tender the seasoned, beaten egg is poured into the pan. This *pipérade* when half-cooked is turned over and cooked on the other side. It is served flat. *Pipérade basquaise* is always cooked solely in oil.

Pistou. A Mediterranean sauce very like Italian *pesto*. It is made from garlic, tomato purée, basil, and cheese pounded together while oil is dripped into it – rather like a mayonnaise. When prepared this is poured into a hot spring vegetable soup called *soupe au pistou*. This is composed of whatever is around in the market in spring.

Pocher. To poach, i.e. cook very gently in water. See *frémir*.

Poêle. A pan like a frying-pan. Cooking *à la poêle* is more often done in a covered pan in the oven than in a *poêle*, oddly enough.

Poêle, à la. Cooked in butter at a lower rate than sauté. This is usually a menu way of describing food cooked *étuvée*.

Pointe de culotte. See *pièce de bœuf*.

Potages. Soups. Here are the basic groups. Names are often incorrectly used even on menus:

Thick soups.

Purée. Starchy vegetable base.

Velouté. Purée enriched with cream and egg yolk.

Crème. Creamy (e.g. shellfish) soups with a *béchamel* base.

Clear soups.

Potage. Unthickened soup with meat, vegetables, etc.

Consommé. Clear broth.

Pot-au-feu. Beef (*bouilli*), vegetables and broth cooked together but served separately. See page 130.

Potée. Stew-like soup of pork, cabbage, and sausage.

Praline. Toasted almonds and caramelized sugar blended.

Pré-salé. From '*les prés-salés*', the salty northern grasslands; a fine recommendation for lamb or mutton.

Quenelles. Lightweight dumplings of meat or fish used as a garnish for meat, fish, or soup. A highly esteemed delicacy considered a difficult test of the cook's skill.

Quiches. Savoury open tarts, almost always with egg as part of the filling. The fillings served without pastry (i.e. in a *gratin* dish) are called *gratins*.

Rafraîchir. Refresh; plunge hot food into cold water (see page 116).

Ravigote. A piquant sauce (see page 140).

Réduire. Reduce in bulk by rapid boiling (see page 118).

Rémoulade. A mayonnaise plus capers, anchovy, tarragon, chervil, onion, gherkins (see page 138).

Render. Obtain fat by heating gently for long period.

Rognonnade. A loin of meat when kidneys are included. Sometimes the whole thing is boned and rolled. (Page 178 shows how it looks.)

Romsteck. Rump steak.

Rosbif. Roast beef.

Roux. Fat and flour mixed over heat until the flour is cooked.

Sabayon. See *zabaglione*.

Saindoux. Rendered down pork fat, what we would call lard. Good for making pastry. More about cooking fats on pages 48–9.

Salmis. Game or meat cooked almost through, then given a final cooking at the dinner table.

Salpicon. Pieces of meat or fish or vegetable held in a sauce. Used to make croquettes or fill *vol-au-vents* or *canapés*.

Saucisse. Sausage; needs cooking.

Saucisson. Sausage; already cooked.

Sauté. Fried in very little fat. Pan is usually 'sautoir', an open frying-pan. See *poêle* and page 180.

Savarin. A cake made with yeast dough served soaked in rum, etc. A *baba* is the same cake with raisins in the dough.

Scald. Bring almost to boiling point. Sometimes it is boiling water poured on to things.

S.G. Menu sign – *selon grosseur* – price according to size.

Sommelier. Wine waiter.

Soubise. An onion sauce or purée of onion and rice. See page 126.

Soupe. Peasant soup laden with vegetables and usually bread. Peasants say, 'I'm going to have the soup' when they go to have their meal.

Stew. Meat cooked by the circulation of water. It is therefore always cooked on a stove-top and the liquid must be free to move around. For this reason it's usually cut-up meat, although if the liquid is free to move around it, one large piece of meat can be described as a stew. If the stew is a thick one (hot-pot is a better word for it), it's best to cook it *étuvée* or in a double-boiler so that the heat won't scorch the bottom of the pan and cause it to stick.

Table wine. Still wine with less than 14 per cent alcohol.

Tartare. A mayonnaise started from hard egg-yolks instead of raw ones, then finished like a *rémoulade*

Tartare, à la. Raw beef, ground and garnished with

capers, chopped onion, parsley, and a raw egg-yolk. All eaten raw. See page 190.

Tendron. A cut of meat (veal) which includes false ribs. Highly thought of in France because it gives a gelatinous crunchy stew. English middle section of breast corresponds.

Terrine. Chopped or ground meat (sometimes, though rarely, fish) baked in a *terrine* dish. If the meat is enclosed in pastry this becomes a *pâté*. *Pâté* can be served hot or cold, *terrine* is always served cold.

Timbale. Any preparation served in piecrust.

Tournedos. Slices of fillet of beef weighing about 100 grams ($3\frac{1}{2}$ oz.). *Médaillons*, *noisettes*, and *mignonnettes* are exactly the same, used merely to jazz up the menu.

York Ham. In France this merely means a cooked ham as distinct from the hams that are eaten raw.

Zabaglione. Dessert made by whipping egg and alcohol over low heat, can be eaten hot or cold. This is called *sabayon* in France; both French and Italian versions are very old recipes. See page 210.

LE MENU, PLANNING IT

In the first half of the nineteenth century the host and cook didn't face the problems of planning. Everything was put out on the table in one big heap and the guests sorted it out where they liked.

This is still done with the buffet supper, but stand-up parties cannot compare with dinner parties, however simple the dinner. Even at buffet parties, hot courses should be served, preferably at pre-planned times. The Edwardian dinner was quite an event for those who could afford it, and those who could digest it. Nowadays such feasts are very rare indeed and this sort of menu is a collector's item.

* Hors d'œuvre
(perhaps oysters)

Soup (thick or clear)

Fish (probably poached and plain)

* Entrée (often very complex dish)

* Relevé (a really big joint – the barons and saddles now no longer seen)

Rôti (game or poultry)

Vegetables

Sweet (perhaps a trifle or a tipsy pudding)

Savoury (often hot, e.g. anchovy on toast)

Cheese

Dessert (nuts and fresh fruit)

* These courses at a formal dinner.

More and more people are following the French menu, which brings the cheese course on before the cooked sweet (now called dessert), and always finds some sort of simple salad to follow the vegetables. A first-rate modern dinner party might serve something like this:——

Careful choice means that a large menu need be neither expensive nor troublesome. After all, your guests will only eat until they are sick. Whether they hit you for enormous helpings of two courses, or tiny helpings of eight courses, need not affect your budget. In other words, many courses call for tiny helpings.

Don't have two courses that are in a thick sauce. Don't follow a thick soup with a stew. Consider colour, texture, and heat.

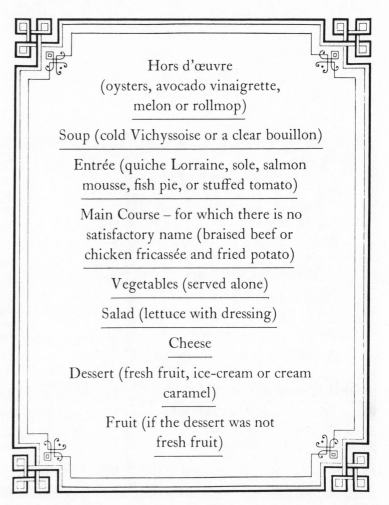

Hors d'œuvre
(oysters, avocado vinaigrette, melon or rollmop)

Soup (cold Vichyssoise or a clear bouillon)

Entrée (quiche Lorraine, sole, salmon mousse, fish pie, or stuffed tomato)

Main Course – for which there is no satisfactory name (braised beef or chicken fricassée and fried potato)

Vegetables (served alone)

Salad (lettuce with dressing)

Cheese

Dessert (fresh fruit, ice-cream or cream caramel)

Fruit (if the dessert was not fresh fruit)

À la Carte

HOW TO SAY IT AND KNOW WHAT YOU'RE GETTING

À la VAPEUR (a lah vapp-urr) - steamed.
POCHÉ (posh-ay) - poached.
POÊLÉ (po-ell-ay) - shallow fried.
FRIT (free) - deep fried.
À la MEUNIÈRE (a lah murr-nee-air) - cooked slowly in butter.
SAURÉ (soar-ay) - fried or smoke cured.

YOUR STEAK CAN BE:

BLEU (blur) - very rare.
SAIGNANT (say-nee-on) - rare.
À POINT (a pwun) - medium.
BIEN CUIT (bee-yun kwee) - well done.

JULIENNE (jooly-enn)
— veg. cut like matchsticks.
MACÉDOINE (massay-dwun)
— veg. or fruit size of beans.
FARÇI (far-see) - stuffed.
Flambé (flom-bay) - all on fire.
PANÉ (pan-ay) - breadcrumb covering.
FRANÇAISE (fron-says)
— cooked in butter.
Anglaise (ong-lays)
— cooked in steam or water.
ITALIENNE (ee-tally-enn)
— paste & tomatoes.
RUSSE (rooss) - sour cream.
ALLEMANDE (allur-mond) - mit sauerkraut.
Flamande (flamm-ond) - endive.
INDIENNE (ahn-dee-enn)
— rice or curry.
Mexicaine (mexi-cayn) - pimento.

PORTUGAISE (port-you-gaze)
— tomato, onion, oil.
ESPAGNOLE (ess-pan-yoll) - onion.
Hongroise (ong-wahs) - paprika.
AUTRICHIENNE (o-trishee-enn)
— sweet sauce.
MALTAISE (mall-tays) - oranges.
HOLLANDAISE (oll-on-days)
— eggs used.
ARABE (a-rahb)
CRÉOLE (kray-oll) } rice probably
GRECQUE (grekk)
FLORENTINE (floor-on-teen)
— spinach.
BOHÉMIENNE (bow-aim-ee-enn)
— goulash or sour cream.
MILANAISE (mill-on-ays) - spaghetti.

NOTE: a AS IN CAT WHEN BY ITSELF & ALL VOWELS SHORT WHEN FOLLOWED BY DOUBLE CONSONANT.

PARMENTIER (par-mont-ee-ay) – potato is there.

NORMANDE (nor-mond) – cream sauce.

Périgourdine (perry-goor-dean) – truffles, foie gras.

NIÇOISE (nee-swahs) – tomato, anchovy, garlic, olive.

LYONNAISE (lee-on-ays) – onions.

Provençale (prov-on-sall) – oil, tomato, garlic.

BASQUAISE (bass-kays) – tomato, pimento.

Vichyssoise (vee-she-swahs) – iced leek soup, or a carrot dish.

Sarladaise (sah-lah-days) – truffles.

Rouennaise (roo-on-ays) – duck.

Cancalaise (kon-kah-lays) – oysters.

SOISSONNAISE (swuss-on-ays) – garden produce, especially beans.

DIEPPOISE (dee-epp-wahs) – cream and shrimp.

BERCY (bear-see) – red wine, shallots.

Maconnaise (makk-on-ays) ⎫

BOURGUIGNONNE (boor-gee-nyonn) ⎬ some burgundy wine involved.

CHAMBERTIN (shom-bear-tun) ⎭

DARNE (dahn) – thick slice (esp. fish).

PAUPIETTE (po-pee-ett) – rolled meat slice containing stuffing.

PAPILLOTE (papp-ee-yott) – paper envelope in which meat is cooked.

À la diable (a lah dee-ah-blur) – very hot taste.

POTÉE (pott-ay) – pork hotpot.

FINANCIÈRE (fee-nonn-see-air) – expensive ingredients.

CHARCUTIÈRE (shah-koo-tee-air) – using pork products.

POIVRADE (pwuv-rahd) – peppery.

RAVIGOTE (ravvi-gott) – appetising.

CHASSEUR (shass-urr) ⎫

DIANE (dee-ahn) ⎬ of the hunt.

St HUBERT (sant oo-bear) ⎭

St ANTOINE (sant ann-twun) – pork.

JARDINIÈRE (jar-dinn-ee-air) – fresh veg.

MATELOTE (matt-urr-lott) – sailor style. eg. fish stew.

MARINIÈRE (ma-ree-nee-air) – from the sea.

BLANQUETTE (blonk-ett) – meat in thick white sauce.

FRICANDEAU (free-kan-doe) – fried or stewed meat (esp. veal) in sauce.

NAVARIN (navv-ah-run) – mutton stew + potatoes and turnip.

DAUBE (dorb) – braised meat country style.

FRICASSÉE (free-kass-ay) – generally chicken in egg + cream sauce.

BISQUE (beesk) – thick shellfish soup.

SALMIS (sall-mee) – slice game/poultry in sauce.

LA BATTERIE DE CUISINE

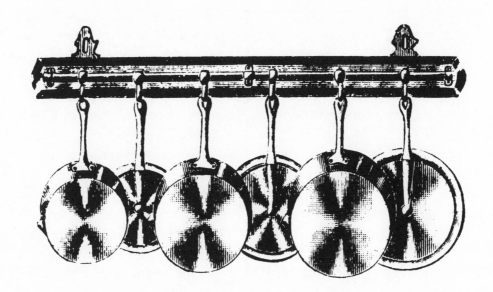

Use any sort of materials you like. Watch that they are good and heavy and go for the rather dreary-looking well-made professional sort, not the bright coloured one with the dodgy-looking plastic handle. ENAMELLED IRON is heavy and a good heat-conductor but it will chip and scratch if knocked about. If well looked after, an enamelled iron frying-pan is great for making omelettes.

IRON is a classic. Heavy black iron pots are my favourite type of utensil but they must be dried carefully or they will rust.

COPPER is heavy and a superb conductor of heat, especially if you get old pots with hand-set bottoms. The tin lining will melt if the pot boils dry and you will have to have it retinned – not very expensive – because otherwise it will discolour the food. But properly made copper pans have now become very rare. Most on sale are simply a foil-thin layer of copper put over an inferior metal to make it look like a copper pan.

HEAVY ALUMINIUM is a good all-round material. It will take quite a beating if the pan is well-made and heavy but avoid the thin dent-easy kind. However, neither iron nor aluminium is suitable for egg-yolk or wine and it's not a good idea to leave cold food standing around in such pots. But then it's not a good idea to leave food standing around in any metal pots.

NON-STICK PANS have a silicone surface. Useful for omelettes and scrambled eggs but all too often the pans that have this sort of surface are thin and shoddily made. In any case the silicone surface will wear away no matter how carefully you treat it.

CERAMIC. There are some fantastic heat-resisting ceramics that are worth investigating. Not so long ago I saw someone deep-frying over a gas flame in a Pyrex dish that was given free with two packs of detergent. Several sorts of Continental earthenware will take direct gas flame but it's worth having an asbestos mat to spread the heat evenly because these ceramics make hot-spots. No pan will benefit from rapid changes of temperature; don't put a hot pan into cold water.

The non-stainless type of knife is best for the kitchen. The simplest way to sharpen them is to use a very fine-tooth file, then give the knife a few strokes on a good cook's-steel. Keep your knives clean and dry. Use them only upon a wooden surface.

If possible the oven should be able to apply very

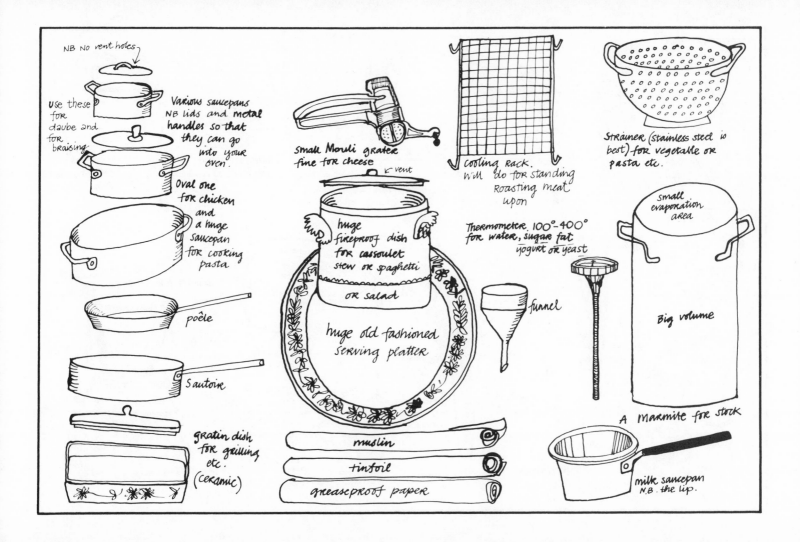

NB No vent holes

Use these for daube and for braising

Various saucepans NB lids and metal handles so that they can go into your oven.

Oval one for chicken and a huge saucepan for cooking pasta

poêle

sautoir

gratin dish for grilling etc. (ceramic)

small Mouli grater fine for cheese

← vent

huge fireproof dish for cassoulet stew or spaghetti

or salad

huge old fashioned serving platter

muslin

tinfoil

greaseproof paper

cooling rack. Will do for standing Roasting meat upon

Thermometer 100°-400° for water, sugar fat yogurt or yeast

funnel

Strainer (stainless steel is best) for vegetable or pasta etc.

small evaporation area

Big volume

A Marmite for stock

milk saucepan N.B. the lip.

lifter

Flexible palette knife - spatula

Loose base

NB. Ridge.

English/U.S. type

French flan Ring
sits on baking tray
(there's no base)

chopping board

Another pie case

individual dishes
for onion soup...

scale for larger weights
[up to 7 lbs.]

...or eggs
very luxe!

Chinois
must be
stainless
steel.

6 small skewers
for fixing
joints

balance for smaller
more
exact
weights
(up to
16 ozs.)

MOULIN-LÉGUMES

Food mill
(moulin)

with
various
size
strainers

A terrine - will double as
a casserole

pepper mill

salt grinder

8
fancy flat
skewers for cooking
kebab etc. (Bicycle
spokes will do!)

Dredger for
sprinkling flour

Flour

forcing bag for
cream choux paste
or potato.

transparent
measuring jug

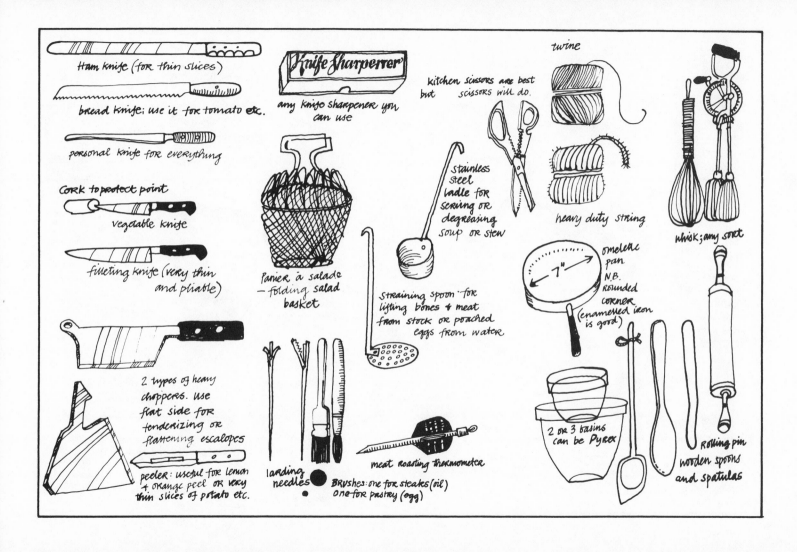

Ham knife (for thin slices)

bread knife; use it for tomato etc.

personal knife for everything

Cork to protect point

vegetable knife

filleting knife (very thin and pliable)

2 types of heavy choppers. use flat side for tenderizing or flattening escalopes

peeler: useful for lemon + orange peel or very thin slices of potato etc.

Knife Sharperrer

any knife sharpener you can use

Panier à salade — folding salad basket

larding needles

BRUSHES: one for steaks (oil) one for pastry (egg)

kitchen scissors are best but scissors will do.

Stainless steel ladle for serving or degreasing soup or stew

Straining spoon for lifting bones & meat from stock or poached eggs from water

meat roasting thermometer

twine

heavy duty string

omelette pan N.B. rounded corner (enamelled iron is good)

2 or 3 basins can be Pyrex

whisk; any sort

Rolling pin

wooden spoons and spatulas

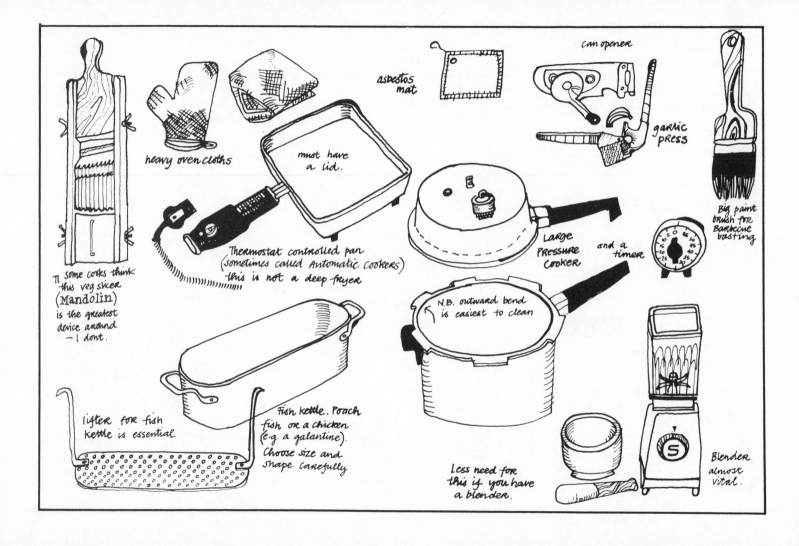

heavy oven cloths

asbestos mat

can opener

garlic press

must have a lid.

Big paint brush for Barbecue basting

Thermostat controlled pan (sometimes called Automatic Cookers) this is not a deep fryer

Large Pressure Cooker

and a timer

π Some cooks think this veg slicer (Mandolin) is the greatest device around — I dont.

N.B. outward bend is easiest to clean

lifter for fish kettle is essential

Fish kettle. Poach fish or a chicken (e.g. a galantine). Choose size and shape carefully

Less need for this if you have a blender.

Blender almost vital.

low heat, e.g. 200° F., as these low heats are kindest to most foods. Failing that, be sure to have a metal tin – *bain-marie* – in which a terrine or pot can stand.

I'd say an electric machine is worth having in any kitchen. It's important that it has enough power to do the work, e.g. a lightweight machine will beat egg-whites but will just burn out trying to knead bread. The large Kenwood can handle any job. I have found the most useful attachments to be the blender, coffee grinder, meat grinder, dough hook, and the potato peeler, which is especially useful for large quantities. The ordinary mixing device 'rubs in' fat and flour for pastry making very efficiently, which endears it to me since that's a job I don't like.

A kitchen table is the final kitchen utensil. My dining table is a huge bench marked by chisel, drill, and dog-end. It's used for chopping vegetables, boning meat, and rolling pastry, then it's washed down and the places set for dinner. The great advantage of eating off bare wood is that very hot casseroles can be put directly on to the table, bread can be sliced without a bread-board and if a guest spills a little wine on it or adds a little *graffito* no one even notices.

LA CARTE DES SAUCES

A guide through the complex world of the *chef saucier*.
These charts should give you enough facts to make any of the sauces listed.

ABBREVIATIONS

T=Tablespoon   t=teaspoon   bg=*bouquet garni*   * serve it with any of these
S=seasoning, basically pepper and salt. Adjust flavour to suit your taste

CHART N° 1 : BROWN SAUCES

FONDS BRUN (Rich Brown Stock) Water to cover 3 lb. beef + 2 lb. veal bones. Simmer 3 hours. Add carrot, onion, leek. Sbg. Simmer 1½ hours. Strain. Cool. Degrease. Use this stock to make Demi Glaze. Use the meat and bones again to make *glace de viande*.

DEMI GLAZE Pour 2½ pints *fonds brun* on to a brown *roux* while stirring. Add 2 T tomato purée and 2 T *mirepoix*. Sbg. Simmer 2 hrs. Skim often. Degrease. Use to make other sauces.

ROMAINE Caramelize 2 T sugar. Add 4 T vinegar and reduce to half its volume. Add ½ pint Demi Glaze; simmer 15 minutes. Before serving add 1½ oz. currants, 1½ oz. chopped nuts (almonds or pine kernels). *Tongue or braised veal.

GLACE DE VIANDE Cover bones + meat with cold water. Simmer 5 hours. Strain. Reduce rapidly until you have a thick, dark treacle. Cool. Use this treacle like meat extract.

BEURRE COLBERT Mash 1 T *glace de viande* into 4 oz. soft butter, add a pinch of parsley and tarragon, and 1 t lemon juice. *Lukewarm on grilled meat, roast chicken or fish. Fried fish becomes *à la Colbert* when served this way.

ITALIENNE Cook ham, mushrooms and shallots in oil. To a cupful of that add a cupful of any dry wine and reduce it to half its volume over a high heat. Add 2 cupfuls of Demi Glaze + 1 T tomato purée (home-made if possible) + chopped parsley. Season it, simmer 15 mins. *Liver, eggs, red meat.

LYONNAISE
Cook a small chopped onion in a little butter. Add 8 oz. dry wine and/or vinegar and reduce to half volume. Add $\frac{1}{2}$ pint Demi Glaze.
*Meat or vegetables (v. good with artichoke).

POIVRADE
Cook *mirepoix*. Add $\frac{1}{4}$ pint vinegar $+ \frac{1}{4}$ pint red wine. Reduce by half. Add $\frac{1}{2}$ pint Demi Glaze and 6 crushed pepper corns. Simmer 1 hour. Skim and strain it. If possible add 1 T redcurrant jelly.
*Game.

MADÈRE
Reduce $\frac{1}{2}$ pint Madeira to half its volume. Add $\frac{3}{4}$ pint Demi Glaze and 1 T butter. S. Stir energetically until butter is absorbed then leave to simmer for 2 mins.
*Steak, ham, kidneys, veal, or duck.

PÉRIGUEUX
Cook 2 T diced truffles in a little butter. Add $\frac{1}{2}$ pint *sauce Madère*.
*Pheasant, brains, any red meat.

FINANCIÈRE
Demi Glaze+chicken stock with trimmings of truffle and chopped mushroom. Add a little Madeira that has been reduced by boiling to half its volume.
*With red meat or game.

CHART № 2 :
BÉCHAMEL SAUCES

AUX ŒUFS DURS
Béchamel + 2 finely chopped hard-boiled eggs + handful chopped parsley. S.
*Fish, especially cod.

NANTUA
As *crevette*, substituting crayfish shell.
*Fish.

CREVETTE
Pound shrimp skins with butter. Stir into *béchamel* and boil it up. Strain through cloth. S. If you haven't got enough shrimp skins to make the sauce go pink, add a drip of artificial colouring.
*Shrimps, white fish, or eggs.

BÉCHAMEL
2 oz. butter + 2 oz. flour stirred over low heat 3 mins without browning it. Slowly add 1 pint warm milk. Simmer 3 mins. S.

CARDINAL
As *crevette*, substituting lobster shell.
*Lobster.

RICH CARDINAL
Cardinal + lobster meat and truffles.
*Fish.

CRÈME
To the *béchamel* add ¼ pint warm cream. S.
*Boiled fish, plain veg., poultry, or eggs.

AURORA
Béchamel + 1 T tomato purée + 1 T butter. S.
*Fish, eggs, or poultry.

MORNAY
To the *béchamel* add 6 oz. grated cheese (Parmesan or Gruyère if possible). Remove from heat and stir well. S using pinch nutmeg, pinch cayenne.
*Almost anything: egg, fish, poultry, veal, or vegetable.

RAVIGOTE
$1\frac{1}{2}$ oz. vinegar + $1\frac{1}{2}$ oz. dry white wine + $\frac{1}{2}$ shallot chopped + 1 piece thyme + pinch fresh pepper + bay leaf. Boil to reduce to half the volume. Strain. Add $\frac{1}{2}$ pint *béchamel* and if possible mushroom essence or water in which mushrooms have cooked (about 3 oz.). Simmer 10 mins then add 2 T butter + 2 T cream. S.
*Eggs, fish, or plainly served chicken.

SOUBISE
Béchamel + 1 lb. chopped onion cooked soft in $\frac{1}{2}$ pint dry white wine. Purée the result through a strainer. Add 3 oz. cream. Beat well. S.
*Lamb, mutton, or veg.

A LA CRÈME
Béchamel + 2 beaten egg yolks. Remove from heat, stir energetically while it thickens up.
*Chicken or fish.

CHART N° 3 : WHITE SAUCES

WHITE STOCK
4 lb. veal and/or whole chicken, turnip, celery, onion and bg. Add 4 pints cold water and simmer 8 hours. Cool and degrease.

ESTRAGON A BLANC
Boil a sprig of fresh tarragon in 5 oz. white stock. Strain and thicken with flour to coating consistency. S.
*Chicken (or, if you use fish *fumet* instead of white stock this can be served with fish).

VELOUTÉ
Make a *roux* (2 oz. butter + 2 oz. flour) without browning it. Add 1 pint hot white stock. Simmer 20 mins.

SUPRÊME
Add $\frac{1}{4}$ pint warm cream to 1 pint *velouté*. S.
*Chicken, lamb, sweetbreads, meat of *pot-au-feu*.

POULETTE
Add to $\frac{1}{2}$ pint *allemande* 1 T chopped parsley and 1 t lemon juice. S.
*Almost any offal.

ALLEMANDE (also called *Blonde* or *Parisienne*).
Reduce 1 pint of *velouté* to $\frac{1}{2}$ pint. Add 2 beaten yolks + knob butter or cream + trace nutmeg and 1 t lemon juice. Stir over low heat until thick. S.
*White meat, fish, light offal (e.g. sweetbreads).

VICTORIA
Reduce $\frac{1}{2}$ pint of dry white wine to half its volume. Add $\frac{1}{2}$ pint *allemande* + chopped mushrooms, lobster coral, and butter.
*White fish.

VILLEROI (a special sauce used to coat food).
Allemande sauce is allowed to go tepid. Food is rolled in this cold *allemande*, then into beaten egg to which a trace of olive oil has been added; then roll into breadcrumbs and fry in deep fat.

CHART N° 4 : FISH SAUCES

NORMANDE
Make a white *roux* from 2 oz.butter + 2 oz. flour. Add 1 pint fish *fumet* (*sole fumet* for perfection) and a small spoonful essence of mushroom (water in which mushrooms have cooked will do).
*Any fish but especially sole or turbot.

RÉGENCE
$\frac{1}{2}$ pint white wine reduced by half. Add 4 oz. chopped mushroom and a chopped truffle, add to either *normande*.
*Sole, halibut, or turbot.

NORMANDE (another version).
Take *normande* above; add 4 oz. of butter and/or cream. Strain. S.
*Any fish as above.

DIEPPOISE
Normande (2nd version) + large handful finely chopped parsley and as many whole cooked shrimps as you can get into it.
*Almost any fish.

CHART N° 5 : EGG-BUTTER SAUCES

MALTAISE
Juice of 1 orange + blanched and very finely chopped outer skin of 2 oranges added to 1 pint *hollandaise*. S.
*Fried sole, plaice, prawns, or asparagus.

BEURRE BLANC
Put 2 oz. white vinegar + 2 oz. dry white wine + 1 T chopped shallots into pan. Boil till it's reduced to 2 T liquid. Cool. Strain. Put into double-boiler and when warm whisk into it ½ lb. unsalted butter in pea-sized pieces. (Don't let it get hot.) Serve warm.
*Fish.

HOLLANDAISE
Put 3 egg yolks + 1 T lemon juice into a double boiler and keep whisking it for 3 minutes. Now begin to add 6 oz. butter in pea-size pieces. Finally add 1 T hot water. S. One final whisking and it's ready.
*Fish, eggs, and expensive vegetables.

MOUSSELINE
Put ¼ pint of thick beaten cream into ¾ pint *hollandaise*. S. Serve immediately.
*Fish, asparagus, or salmon cutlet.

FOYOT
2 T *glace de viande* warmed and stirred into 1 pint *béarnaise*.
*Sweetbreads, egg, or light meats.

BÉARNAISE
Put 2 oz. vinegar + 2 oz. dry white wine + 1 T chopped onion + 1 T chopped tarragon in a pan. Boil till it is reduced to 2 T. Strain it and use in place of the lemon juice in the *hollandaise* recipe.
*Steak, grilled chicken, or boiled fish.

COLBERT (compare *beurre Colbert* in Brown Sauces).
Melt 1 T *glace de viande* in 2 T dry white wine. Simmer for 5 mins. Stir into 1 pint *béarnaise*.
*Chicken, steak, or eggs.

CHORON
Put 6 oz. tomato purée (home-made if possible) into 1 pint *béarnaise*. S.
*Steak, fish, chicken, or eggs.

CHART N° 6 : OIL-EGG SAUCES

VERTE
Purée chervil, tarragon, spinach, and watercress for about 5 minutes, then sieve it. Use this to colour mayonnaise.
*Cold food especially if it's well decorated.

MAYONNAISE
Beat 3 egg yolks + 1 T vinegar + a pinch of salt, pepper, and mustard. Drip $\frac{3}{4}$ pint of warm oil into it while still beating.
*Many varieties of cold food from hard boiled eggs to cold fish.

RÉMOULADE
Add chopped capers, gherkins, chervil, tarragon, and onion (anchovy too if you like) to the mayonnaise. Amount is up to you.
*Cold meat, poultry, or lobster.

TARTARE
Use 2 hard yolks + 1 raw one when making mayonnaise. Add ingredients as for *rémoulade*.
*Fried or grilled fish.

TAPÉNADE
$\frac{1}{2}$ pint mayonnaise + 1 T capers + 1 T anchovy and a generous pinch of black pepper.
*Cold boiled beef, cold fish, or hard eggs.

AIOLI
Soak a slice of bread in milk. Pound (or blend) 8 cloves of garlic into it. When it is quite smooth add to raw yolks and proceed as mayonnaise.
*Hot or cold poached fish, stir into hot fish soup, use on cold meat or hot vegetables.

MOHAMMED
2 hard boiled eggs + 3 boned anchovies are chopped together with as much as you like of capers, celery, cucumber, and chopped onion. Add to mayonnaise. S.
*Fish.

CHART N° 7 : HORSERADISH AND OIL-VINEGAR SAUCES

RAIFORT
Mix 1 T grated horseradish + 1 t fresh breadcrumbs that have been soaked in milk. Add same volume of thick cream. Stir. S using mixed English mustard and vinegar in small amounts till it tastes the way you like it.
*Roast beef or steaks.

VINAIGRETTE
2 T vinegar + 6 T olive oil. S using pinch mustard. Stir well.
*Cold vegetables, salad, etc.

MOUTARDE
Into *vinaigrette* mix 1 T French mustard + 2 T boiling water. Stir. Add squeeze lemon juice and 1 t chopped parsley.
*Meat of *pot-au-feu* or any cold beef.

RAVIGOTE
Add 2 T finely chopped herbs (e.g. chives, parsley, chervil), 1 t chopped onion + 1 t capers. S to *vinaigrette*.
*Meat of *pot-au-feu*, cold pig feet, boiled chicken, or boiled fish.

LES LEGUMES SECS, RIZ ET PÂTES

There are dozens of different dried beans. There are large, small, brown, green, white, and black-eyed ones. None of them need be soaked overnight. Two hours' soaking in cold water should be quite enough. Wash them and pick out the damaged or discoloured ones, then put them into a pan with plenty of cold water. If you want to flavour the water this is the time to do it, half an onion is better than nothing at all, stock will make them delicious. Whatever you put with them you must add a small piece of fat. Ham fat for preference but a dab of dripping is O.K. This has an important effect upon the beans, so don't miss it out.

If you intend to serve the beans whole with butter, cream, tomato purée, chopped fried bacon, etc. then they should be cooked until just tender. It's impossible to say how long that will be, it depends upon how large the beans are and how long they have been stored, but two hours is about the average.

Split peas are the inside part of whole dried peas and tiny golden-coloured lentils are the inside part of the larger 'brown lentils'. Of these four only whole dried peas need to be soaked before cooking.

Any dried vegetable of this kind can be mashed to a thick purée (lentils become *dhal*, peas pease pudding) or diluted to become a soup (see page 122).

Rice is a grain and is treated differently from the other dried things. Don't soak it but do wash it very well indeed. Spend at least five minutes changing the water and holding it, in a sieve, under running water. This removes all the mill flour. Put the washed rice into a pan with enough water (or stock) to cover it by $\frac{1}{4}$ inch. Bring the water to the boil as quickly as possible. Stir once to be sure no grains are stuck to the bottom, turn flame *as low as possible*, cover with a well-fitting lid. After twenty minutes turn the heat off. Leave for another five or ten minutes, then serve it. If any rice grains are sticking to the pan you didn't wash it enough. This rice is ready to eat and needs no further treatment. N.B. Basmati rice and wild rice are special types of rice and grass needing different cooking times.

Lastly *pasta*. There are hundreds of varieties. They range from hair-like threads to sheets of *lasagne*. Freshly-made *paste* can be bought in some shops; they are much more delicious than the harder commercially made ones and well worth breaking diet for.

The secret of cooking *pasta* is to have gigantic amounts of fast-boiling water. Fresh *pasta* will take about five minutes, package *pasta* more like fifteen, for the thicker stuff even twenty. Drain it and serve on to hot plates. Serve *pasta* with butter and Parmesan cheese and freshly ground pepper or serve it with cream, tomato *coulis* or chopped anchovy, bacon, etc. Serve it any way you like, you only get fat once.

50 COOKSTRIPS

The basic essentials of weights and measures

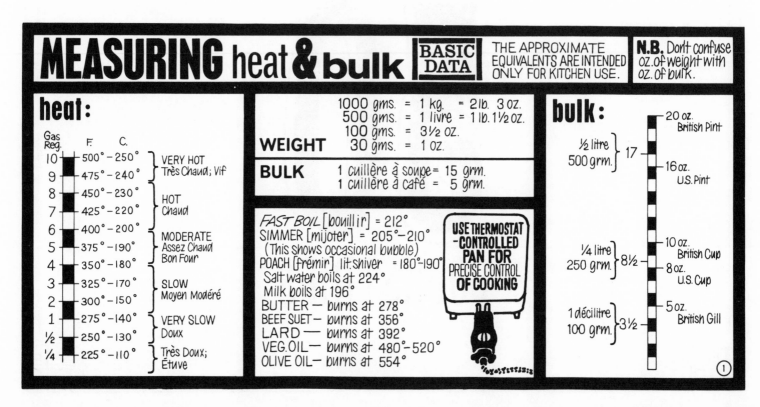

MEASURING heat & bulk | BASIC DATA | THE APPROXIMATE EQUIVALENTS ARE INTENDED ONLY FOR KITCHEN USE. | **N.B.** Don't confuse oz. of weight with oz. of bulk.

heat:

Gas Reg.	F.	C.	
10	500°	250°	VERY HOT Très Chaud; Vif
9	475°	240°	
8	450°	230°	HOT Chaud
7	425°	220°	
6	400°	200°	MODERATE Assez Chaud Bon Four
5	375°	190°	
4	350°	180°	
3	325°	170°	SLOW Moyen Modéré
2	300°	150°	
1	275°	140°	VERY SLOW Doux
½	250°	130°	
¼	225°	110°	Très Doux; Étuve

WEIGHT
1000 gms. = 1 kg. = 2 lb. 3 oz.
500 gms. = 1 livre = 1 lb. 1½ oz.
100 gms. = 3½ oz.
30 gms. = 1 oz.

BULK
1 cuillère à soupe = 15 grm.
1 cuillère à café = 5 grm.

FAST BOIL [bouillir] = 212°
SIMMER [mijoter] = 205°–210°
(This shows occasional bubble)
POACH [frémir] lit. shiver = 180°–190°
Salt water boils at 224°
Milk boils at 196°
BUTTER — burns at 278°
BEEF SUET — burns at 356°
LARD — burns at 392°
VEG. OIL — burns at 480°–520°
OLIVE OIL — burns at 554°

USE THERMOSTAT-CONTROLLED PAN FOR PRECISE CONTROL OF COOKING

bulk:

½ litre 500 grm.	17	20 oz. British Pint
		16 oz. U.S. Pint
¼ litre 250 grm.	8½	10 oz. British Cup
		8 oz. U.S. Cup
1 décilitre 100 grm.	3½	5 oz. British Gill

①

Heat, bulk, and time are of course the three fundamentals of cooking food. Everything else concerns the preparation of food. To cook food (for instance a piece of meat) it is necessary to raise the centremost part of it to a certain temperature. The centre of beef must be between 140° and 170° F. according to how you like it. Lamb and mutton between 145° and 170°, veal 175°, poultry 180°. To measure the temperature at the centre it is best to use a meat thermometer, which is a thick skewer-like implement that is pushed deep into the meat and left there. It must not touch bone or this will throw the reading off. Most recipes assume that you don't have a meat thermometer and so give you an idea of how long to leave the meat in the oven according to its weight, but the shape of the joint makes a difference because a thin flat joint cooks more quickly than a cube shape of the same weight.

For this reason a stew consisting of equal-sized cubes of meat will take the same time to cook whether there is a total of 1 lb. or 4 lbs. of meat.

Boiling point is one temperature that the cook can see without any special apparatus, so it's lucky that the boiling point of water, 212° F., is such a crucial temperature. Meat cooked in liquid that is boiling hardens; so stews must be kept below boiling point and must never bubble. Meat or vegetable cooked in a closed container at below boiling point is described as *à l'étuvée* (see lowest oven temperature), appearing on menus as *à la poêle*. Because this is a very long process meat cooked this way is usually cut into small cubes. Any of the braised vegetable recipes I have given can be cooked *étuvée*; it is especially succulent and flavourful. For best results put plenty of butter into the pot before cooking. At this temperature it can't burn.

The sign of a professional chef is evenly cut vegetables

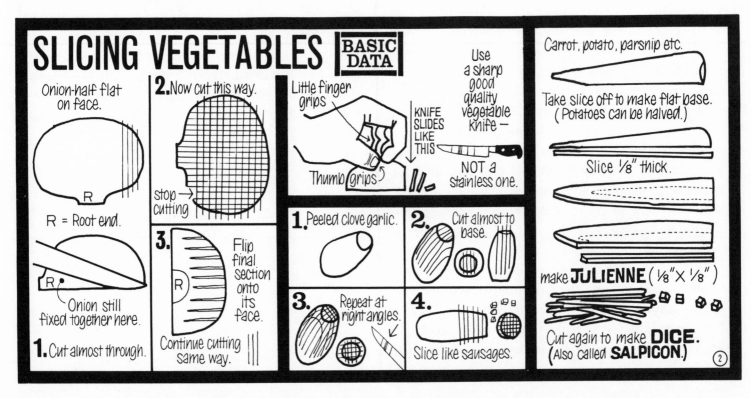

SLICING VEGETABLES BASIC DATA

Onion-half flat on face.

R = Root end.

Onion still fixed together here.

1. Cut almost through.

2. Now cut this way.

stop → cutting

3. Flip final section onto its face.

Continue cutting same way.

Little finger grips

KNIFE SLIDES LIKE THIS

Thumb grips

Use a sharp good quality vegetable knife —

NOT a stainless one.

1. Peeled clove garlic.

2. Cut almost to base.

3. Repeat at right angles.

4. Slice like sausages.

Carrot, potato, parsnip etc.

Take slice off to make flat base. (Potatoes can be halved.)

Slice ⅛" thick.

make **JULIENNE** (⅛" × ⅛")

Cut again to make **DICE**. (Also called **SALPICON**.)

②

It's a delight to watch an expert cook chopping an onion. The rounded point end of the knife is used to rock the blade down on to the fast-moving onion as I have drawn in the second half of section one. By leaving the root end attached the onion is manageable until the very last cut. Cutting a clove of garlic, it's important that the pieces are as tiny as possible so that you don't get a piece in your mouth when eating the finished dish. The whole bulb of garlic is called a 'head' and in some parts of the world the clove is called a 'tooth' and the roots are called the 'beard'. Well-cut vegetables end up with all the pieces of equal size, so that the pieces will be equally cooked in the final result. This is especially important with fried potatoes. Potato cut into *julienne* strips need be fried only once (large chips are best fried twice– the second time merely to crisp them) but should they be uneven you will end up with lots of black ones that you will have to pick over.

When onions are used as a garnish it is best to use the smaller varieties but the large ones can have their outer layers taken off. They will look superb if glazed. Glazing is usually done by cooking in an open pan so that the water is evaporated away. Skilled cooks judge it just right so that the vegetable is perfectly cooked as the last drop of water hisses into oblivion. You and I might have to add a sly drop of liquid now and again. As the pan gets dryish add a big knob of butter and two or three pinches of sugar. This will go to a goo and the vegetables are rolled into it. Turnips, onions, swedes, and carrots, can be treated like this. On the menu it will say *navets glacés* (glazed turnips) or *oignons glacés* (glazed onions) but carrots are always called *carottes Vichy*.

Flour-based sauce. Preparing and cooking vegetables. Skimming fat

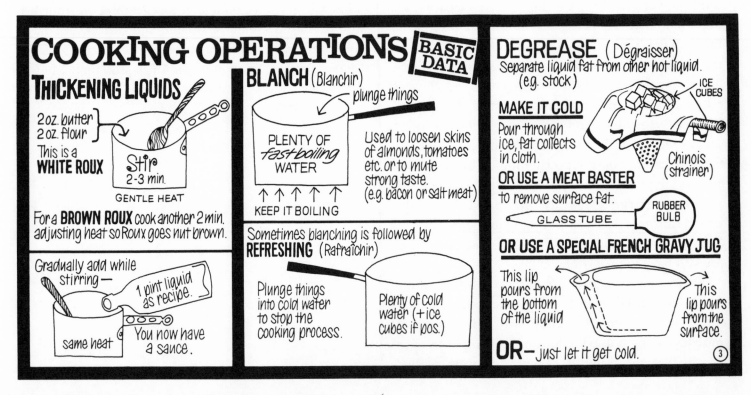

COOKING OPERATIONS [BASIC DATA]

THICKENING LIQUIDS

2 oz. butter
2 oz. flour

This is a **WHITE ROUX**

Stir 2-3 min.

GENTLE HEAT

For a **BROWN ROUX** cook another 2 min. adjusting heat so Roux goes nut brown.

Gradually add while stirring—

1 pint liquid as recipe.

same heat

You now have a sauce.

BLANCH (Blanchir)

plunge things

PLENTY OF *fast-boiling* WATER

KEEP IT BOILING

Used to loosen skins of almonds, tomatoes etc. or to mute strong taste. (e.g. bacon or salt meat)

Sometimes blanching is followed by **REFRESHING** (Rafraîchir)

Plunge things into cold water to stop the cooking process.

Plenty of cold water (+ ice cubes if pos.)

DEGREASE (Dégraisser)

Separate liquid fat from other hot liquid. (e.g. stock)

ICE CUBES

MAKE IT COLD

Pour through ice, fat collects in cloth.

Chinois (strainer)

OR USE A MEAT BASTER

to remove surface fat.

GLASS TUBE

RUBBER BULB

OR USE A SPECIAL FRENCH GRAVY JUG

This lip pours from the bottom of the liquid

This lip pours from the surface.

OR — just let it get cold.

③

A sauce is a thickened liquid. If it is to be thickened with flour it's usual to make a *roux*. There are three kinds of *roux*. A white *roux* is used for *béchamel* or *velouté* type sauce. It enables the cook to preserve the light colour of the result which is so important to it. A brown *roux* is for the dark sauces and dishes, especially for the *espagnole* and *Demi Glaze*, where the rich brown colour is best achieved by the natural caramelizing process rather than by artificial colouring. Between these two there is another *roux*, a blond one. It is a pale gold and is usually cooked more quickly than the others. A *roux* always uses butter and since butter has such a low burning point (see page 112) it must be heated with care. If it doesn't interfere with the recipe the pint of liquid that is added to the *roux* is best hot. This makes the blending of the liquid and the *roux* simpler than if it's cold.

Food is blanched for many different reasons. Tomatoes, peaches, and nuts are treated this way so that the skins are easily removed. Salt can be a menace in cooking and blanching is a way of removing or reducing the saltiness of bacon or pork-fat before rendering it down for cooking. On page 194 I have shown blanching as a way of cooking vegetables.

Parboiling is an English word for the same operation but parboiling implies that the food is in the hot water for a longer period of time.

Degreasing (*dégraisser*) is also the word used to describe cutting the fat away from a piece of meat. As a rule the fat taken from the top of stock is heavily flavoured and can only be used for rather specialized types of cooking. Therefore the cook who tells an assistant to degrease means that the fat should be thrown away. The very simplest way of doing this is to remove any large solids from the stock (i.e. veal knuckle, bones, etc.) then leave it to cool for a few hours. The other methods are only for cooks in a hurry.

Fat: rendering it down, clarifying it

COOKING OPERATIONS — BASIC DATA

Making — **RILLETTES** (which is a rich fatty spread served with dry warm toast) is a good illustration of the "RENDERING of fat." *

1. 2 lb. of PORK BELLY in cubes ½" — ¼ pint water

Low heat 2–3 hrs.

faggot of herbs. clove of garlic generous salt + pepper

* In which case omit flavourings.

2. When all water has gone remove garlic etc.

Drain pieces and tear to shreds.

3. Serve shredded result chilled

RilLettes — Use surplus fat for cooking.

CLARIFY BUTTER

1. Warm butter — Gentle heat

2. Let it get cold — then turn it out.

3. Remove the white sediment. This part is clarified butter

REDUCE (Réduire)

N.B. NO LID!

Boil down liquid over a high flame to increase flavour of remainder.

④

There is nothing more simple than making *rillettes*. The result is a cross between best pork dripping and *terrine*. Any fatty pork can be used, belly or pig-cheek being particularly suitable and very cheap. If you wish, add a little lean rabbit or a little goose (*rillettes* of Le Mans). Carefully remove the *bouquet garni* and any bones. Decide how much fat to put with the shredded meat. Some cooks prefer a very fatty result and others as lean as they can get it, using the fat merely to keep it all together. *Rillettes* must be fatty enough to spread on dry toast. *Rillauds* and *rillons* are made in the same way as *rillettes* except that at the end the lean meat is not shredded. The pieces should in fact be browned and even slightly crisp. *Rillauds* and *rillons* are sometimes served hot. In this case remove as much fat as possible. These recipes cannot be overcooked; if you wish they can be left in the lowest possible oven overnight. They will keep very well in a cool dry place if you put a thin layer of pure lard over the top to seal off any meat particles, and cover with foil.

Clarified butter should be used in all cooking processes that demand butter, especially frying, for it is the impurities that burn most easily. Eggs or chicken breast cooked in butter will be better in every way if the butter is clarified first. If you are in a hurry wait while the sediment settles, then pour off the clear part for use.

The process of reducing liquids is useful to the cook, for it enables him to use generous amounts of liquid to avoid worries about pans boiling dry. Saltiness will obviously increase as the liquid is reduced, so most cooks keep stocks undersalted until the liquid is reduced. Reduce usually means 'reduce to half the original volume'.

Herbs and how to use them

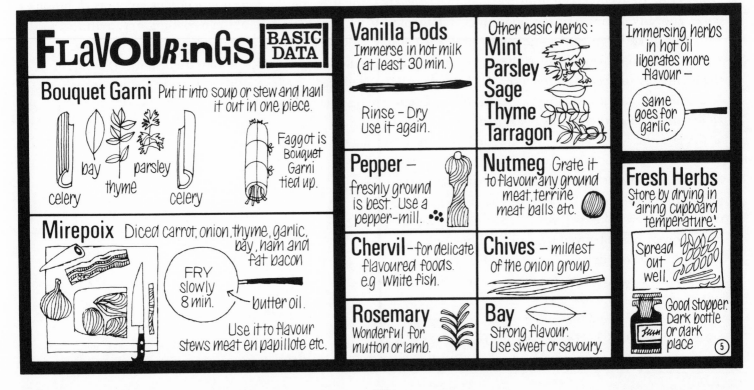

FLaVOURinGS | BASIC DATA

Bouquet Garni Put it into soup or stew and haul it out in one piece.

celery, bay, thyme, parsley, celery

Faggot is Bouquet Garni tied up.

Mirepoix Diced carrot, onion, thyme, garlic, bay, ham and fat bacon

FRY slowly 8 min. — butter oil.

Use it to flavour stews meat en papillote etc.

Vanilla Pods Immerse in hot milk (at least 30 min.)

Rinse – Dry Use it again.

Pepper – freshly ground is best. Use a pepper-mill.

Chervil – for delicate flavoured foods. e.g. White fish.

Rosemary Wonderful for mutton or lamb.

Other basic herbs:
Mint
Parsley
Sage
Thyme
Tarragon

Nutmeg Grate it to flavour any ground meat, terrine meat balls etc.

Chives – mildest of the onion group.

Bay Strong flavour. Use sweet or savoury.

Immersing herbs in hot oil liberates more flavour – same goes for garlic.

Fresh Herbs Store by drying in 'airing cupboard temperature.'

Spread out well.

Good stopper. Dark bottle or dark place

(5)

There's no need to tell you that fresh herbs are a thousand times better than the dried variety, but the ones you dry yourself will certainly be better than the desiccated powder from tins and packets. Luckily celery, which is the anchor man of the *bouquet garni*, is in season throughout the year. Parsley is almost always available too and the French cook looks upon it as a valuable source of flavour and not something to push into a cooked herring's mouth. The *bouquet garni* I have shown is standard form, but vary it according to the food it is associating with. Chervil, rosemary, and basil are often in it and sometimes chunks of lemon or orange peel. A lamb *daube* for instance (page 186) requires orange peel in the marinade and there can be a faggot containing some too if you wish. For fish, fennel (either root, seeds, or feathery leaves) is a superb flavouring.

To obtain maximum flavour from herbs (especially dried herbs) it is best to heat them in a little oil before adding them to liquid, for the high temperature will take the flavour from the herbs. Some cooks at that stage discard the herbs and add only the flavoured oil to the dish they are preparing.

A *mirepoix* is a highly flavoured mixture (or *fondue*) used to add flavour to many dishes from soups to shellfish. In the case of the latter the one used would be *mirepoix au maigre* which contains no bacon or ham. A *mirepoix au gras* can have ham, pork belly, or bacon. A *matignon* is exactly the same thing. Some cooks like to cook such a mixture for a very long time until it becomes a homogeneous pulp. One cook told me that a *matignon* is different from a *mirepoix* because the former should contain a good slug of Madeira, but I think this was just an excuse to pour one for both of us.

Potato soup and some variations on it

Potage Parmentier —is at the root of many FRENCH SOUPS adapted to what is available.

1. Peel, slice and dice 1lb. potatoes.

1lb. leeks.

Include best of green.

3 pints water

SIMMER 45 MIN.

2. Put it through a mouli or mash it with a fork to make a purée.

Taste it and season it. Reheat if necessary.

Mouli

3. Remove from heat. **ADD:** 3oz. Double Cream

STIR.

Scatter chopped chives or parsley on top. — SERVE.

SOME CHANGES TO MAKE

At stage **1.** use stock (e.g. ham bone stock) instead of water.

Use root vegetable (e.g. Turnip, swede, carrot.)

Use (soaked cooked) peas, beans or lentils.

Use watercress for final 15 min. simmering. Puree it with other ingredients. Garnish with chopped watercress for 'Potage au Cresson.'

Serve the stuff cold and call it VICHYSSOISE which is an American variant.

⑥

This is an example of the great family of European purée soups. There is *conti* from lentil purée, *conde* from red bean purée, *savarin* from white bean purée, as well as all the vegetable variations: fresh pea (*St Germain*), carrot (*Crécy*), spinach, etc. The milk and cream moves them from the farmhouse to the restaurant. At the root of them all is the potato, for when Antoine-Auguste Parmentier (1737–1817) introduced and popularized it – by all manner of gimmicks including putting armed soldiers around the crop – the potato changed the history of Europe. The beet gave place to the potato, which was hardier and a more prolific crop. From that time on the potato frontier was pushed farther and farther east until nowadays we associate beet soup with Eastern Poland and Russia.

Potato soup presents the potato in its most digestible form, suitable for old people, infants, or invalids. It is a good diabetic food because it contains far less carbohydrate than bread. Potatoes, like most vegetables, lose their nutritional power to hot water, so either don't cook them in water or use the water as does this soup recipe.

Cauliflower can be substituted for leek to make a cauliflower soup. In this case onion is optional. All these thick soups – but especially the potato – will respond to generous garlic and salt or, if you want to be more adventurous, add caraway seed and lemon peel too. Sour cream or yoghurt can be substituted for the cream into which, for extra thickness, beat an egg yolk or two before pouring it in. The top can be garnished with a scattering of paprika pepper instead of parsley.

How to poach a fish. Making a fish soup

basic stock

FUMET de POISSON au VIN BLANC

This is a simple fumet suitable for poaching a whole fish in. It can also be used as a simple fish soup after straining.

2 lb. cleaned fish (heads are fine) Halibut, Whiting, Flounder etc.

Squeeze lemon.

1 chopped onion.

2 pints water.

Bring to boil. SKIM

½ BOTTLE DRY WHITE WINE

Simmer 45 min.

USE OR SERVE

The fish should be simmered VERY GENTLY in this fumet until tender but not flaking to pieces.

A MORE COMPLEX FISH SOUP

1. Sauté one chopped onion in butter until golden.

2 lb. fish (cleaned boned and in chunks) (Whiting, mackerel cod etc.)

1 clove garlic (crushed)

faggot of herbs. (celery, bay, parsley)

2 pints water.

½ lb. diced potato.

Simmer 25 min.

2. Discard herbs. Serve fish & soup separately.

SOUP

FISH & POTATO

⑦

A fish-flavoured stock can be served as a soup or used when fish is gently poached. It is never boiled, for this would break the fish. Nor is it ever 'poached in butter' which is a piece of menu nonsense that merely means there is a lot of butter on it when it gets to the table. The presence of lemon juice, vinegar, or wine assists in the cooking of the fish, for it also prevents flaking. A piece of juicy lemon rubbed over the fish before cooking it helps still further and will preserve colour and add flavour too. If you are serving a fish cold the fish should be allowed to cool in the *fumet* but as soon as it is cool the fish should be drained or it will deteriorate. In fishing villages salt is scattered generously over cleaned fish even if it will be eaten within an hour. Salt removes any stale odour and keeps the fish in better condition.

Fish cooks very quickly in simmering water or stock. A herring, mackerel, or plaice will probably cook in about ten minutes, trout (of about 7 oz.) a minute or so less, a good-sized sole a little more. This type of stock in the recipe can be used to cook a slice of fish (e.g. cod, halibut, salmon, or skate) or a whole lobster. A lobster weighing two pounds will cook in about 25 minutes.

A fish soup is a very cheap form of protein food. Add bay leaf, carrots, saffron, basil or fennel to the recipe for variants. It's quick to make and easily adapted to many recipes, and yet it is perhaps the weakest part of European cooking as it is practised.

Elegant white sauces

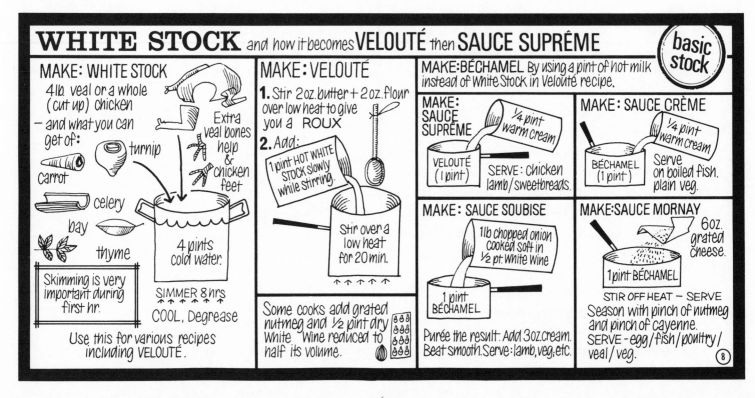

WHITE STOCK and how it becomes VELOUTÉ then SAUCE SUPRÊME

basic stock

MAKE: WHITE STOCK

4 lb. veal or a whole (cut up) chicken

— and what you can get of:

carrot

turnip

celery

bay

thyme

Extra veal bones help & chicken feet

4 pints cold water.

SIMMER 8 hrs
COOL, Degrease

Skimming is very important during first hr.

Use this for various recipes including VELOUTÉ.

MAKE: VELOUTÉ

1. Stir 2 oz. butter + 2 oz. flour over low heat to give you a ROUX
2. Add:

1 pint HOT WHITE STOCK slowly while stirring.

Stir over a low heat for 20 min.

Some cooks add grated nutmeg and ½ pint dry White Wine reduced to half its volume.

MAKE: BÉCHAMEL By using a pint of hot milk instead of White Stock in Velouté recipe.

MAKE: SAUCE SUPRÊME

VELOUTÉ (1 pint)

¼ pint warm cream

SERVE: chicken lamb / sweetbreads.

MAKE: SAUCE CRÈME

BÉCHAMEL (1 pint)

¼ pint warm cream

Serve on boiled fish. plain veg.

MAKE: SAUCE SOUBISE

1 lb chopped onion cooked soft in ½ pt. White Wine

1 pint BÉCHAMEL

Purée the result. Add 3 oz. cream. Beat smooth. Serve: lamb, veg, etc.

MAKE: SAUCE MORNAY

6 oz. grated cheese.

1 pint BÉCHAMEL

STIR OFF HEAT — SERVE

Season with pinch of nutmeg and pinch of cayenne.
SERVE - egg / fish / poultry / veal / veg.

(8)

White stock needs more care than dark stocks because preserving the colour is all-important. Skimming is more important and if you want to cut the amount of skimming back a bit it's a good idea to blanch the veal and chicken and then refresh it. Throw that lot of water away and proceed as in the recipe. This will have removed quite a few of the impurities in one go, but you still must skim at least three times in the first two hours of simmering.

Colour must be preserved when you are making the *roux* for the *velouté*. A little extra heat will darken the flour and your result won't have the bright, light texture that is so important. *Velouté* is not served as a sauce, it's the basis of many sauces. I have given the simplest recipe here but in a restaurant a sauce chef would insist that the *velouté* was simmered for much longer. I remember one chef who didn't think it was worth a damn until it had five hours on a low flame. It is then strained and the surface dabbed with butter. However, after 20 minutes you will have worked quite hard enough and you'll have a pretty good *velouté*. If you want to make a *sauce suprême* from your *velouté*, then the more chicken and the less veal that goes into the original white stock, the more authentic it will be. In the same way it is possible to make a fish *velouté* by pouring a pint of fish *fumet* (see recipe page 124) into the *roux*. This fish *velouté* can then become all sorts of fish sauces. This is why the sauce chef is such an important man in a restaurant. He can take simple items like veal *escalopes*, fish fillets, lamb cutlets and ring a dozen changes on each of them. That's how a restaurant is able to offer you that gigantic menu with its thousand permutations; somewhere below in a great *bain-marie* there are dozens of little saucepans with sauces like these in them.

Making brown stock and meat extract

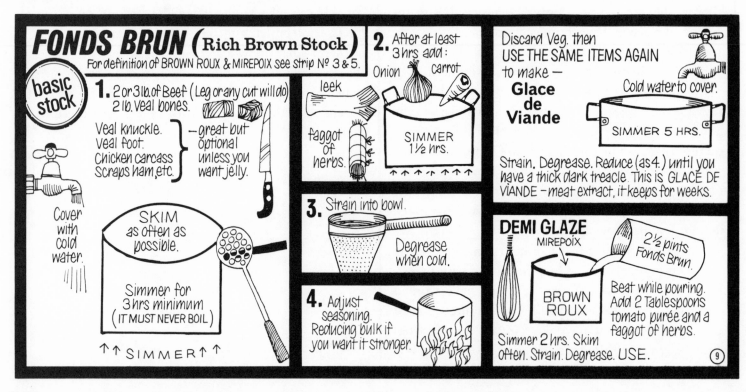

FONDS BRUN (Rich Brown Stock)
For definition of BROWN ROUX & MIREPOIX see strip N° 3 & 5.

basic stock

1. 2 or 3 lb. of Beef (Leg or any cut will do)
2 lb. veal bones.

Veal knuckle.
Veal foot.
Chicken carcass
Scraps ham, etc. } – great but optional unless you want jelly.

Cover with cold water.

SKIM as often as possible.

Simmer for 3 hrs minimum (IT MUST NEVER BOIL)

↑↑ SIMMER ↑↑

2. After at least 3 hrs add:
Onion   carrot
leek
faggot of herbs.
SIMMER 1½ hrs.
↑↑↑↑↑↑

3. Strain into bowl.
Degrease when cold.

4. Adjust seasoning. Reducing bulk if you want it stronger.

Discard Veg. then
USE THE SAME ITEMS AGAIN
to make —
Glace de Viande
Cold water to cover.
SIMMER 5 HRS.

Strain. Degrease. Reduce (as 4.) until you have a thick dark treacle. This is GLACE DE VIANDE – meat extract, it keeps for weeks.

DEMI GLAZE
MIREPOIX
2½ pints Fonds Brun.
BROWN ROUX
Beat while pouring. Add 2 Tablespoons tomato purée and a faggot of herbs.
Simmer 2 hrs. Skim often. Strain. Degrease. USE.
⑨

This is a way to make brown stock; the meat is finally thrown away. If that seems extravagant, take a look at the next cookstrip, which is a variation where the meat is served. I said that white stock needs more care than brown stock in order that it remain white. This is true, but don't make the brown a dumping ground for all the odds and ends around the kitchen. Forget the myths of stock-pots which simmer all the year long and exchange old egg-shells for rich flavoured stock; you will only get out what you put in. Start with a good meaty beginning, add only cold water and never let it boil. Let it get cold as many times as you like, if the heat is too low this is much better than its being too high. In kitchens in which I have worked the stock-pot is cleaned and restarted at least once a week. If you follow the recipe below I suggest you discard the meat, bones, etc. after you have used it to make both the *fonds brun* and the *glace de viande*. For ways of using these things see the sauce chart, pages 96, 97.

A pressure cooker can be used for the first 45 minutes. It will still need simmering for at least two hours and because of the violent action of the pressure cooker it will not go completely clear (which doesn't matter unless you are making a *consommé* or an aspic). The five 'don'ts' of stock making are these:

1. Don't let it boil.
2. Don't use pork or lamb.
3. Don't use starchy vegetables (such as potato).
4. Don't let it cool with the lid on.
5. Don't forget to bring it to boiling point every day.

You can break rule 5 if the stock contains no vegetable matter or if it's kept in the refrigerator. Refrigerated stock need be brought to the boil only every third day.

Glace de viande, if it's reduced to the hard rubber consistency that it should be, will keep for ages. The outside may discolour in spots but this does not indicate that it's spoiled – just remove the spots before using it.

A delicious dinner, a superb soup, and a great sauce

Pot-au-Feu [BASIC SAUCE]

Usually served with more than one sauce. e.g. Moutarde & Ravigote (Strip 15)

Make like FONDS BRUN * using better beef. e.g. Shoulder Topside or Brisket and adding a small white cabbage to the vegetables.

Ladle fat off before serving.

Soup first.

Sliced meat (bouilli) and sliced veg.

SAUCE SUPRÊME (made from this stock) is sometimes served separately.

Petite Marmite

THE ULTIMATE SOUP OF FRENCH COOKING.

As FONDS BRUN * using a nice piece of beef and any of these

3 lb. piece of lean pork.
Boiling chicken.
2 lb. lightly smoked sausage.
Chicken giblets + feet
Marrow bones.
Oxtail sections.

Test for tenderness. Anything cooking too quickly is speared out and returned later. DEGREASE. Discard any non edibles before serving.

Serve as Pot-au-Feu.

Sauce Madère

For steak, ham, veal or egg dishes.

½ pint madeira

REDUCE TO

HALF VOLUME

Add ¾ pint DEMI GLAZE.* Season if needed. Beat in 2 tablespoons butter. SERVE.

* Note : These recipes depend upon FONDS BRUN. (Brown Stock) + DEMI GLAZE(its sauce) Both detailed in strip N° 9.

(10)

This is a meal; the result is a large piece of boiled beef which is sliced and served hot, together with the broth in which it was cooked. Long cooking – about 4 hours – is the secret. There is a part of neck of beef which is called in France *macreuse à pot-au-feu*, but there are many other cuts equally suitable. Topside and thick flank are English cuts corresponding to French choices for this dish. Since with *pot-au-feu* (unlike *fonds brun*) you are going to serve the meat, you should choose an attractive piece, and it should be cooked until tender but not cooked to extinction. *Pot-au-feu* is the pride of the French housewife, who has never cared much for roast joints. There are all sorts of personal variations on this dish, including veal, pork, mutton, duck, and turkey; *pot-au-feu albigeois* is more like a *cassoulet*, having in it raw ham, veal knuckle, haricot beans, goose *pâté*, and slices of sausage. Other recipes concentrate upon the poultry. Sometimes the chicken is stuffed with sausage-meat before putting it into the pot and sometimes the chicken is roasted completely and only put into the *bouillon* a short time before serving. Sliced marrow bones are often cooked in the *bouillon* for the last twenty minutes, then the marrow is taken out and spread on hot toast which is eaten as an accompaniment. The marrow bones might cloud the *bouillon* though. Other accompaniments to the hot sliced meat include gherkins, sea salt (*gros sel*), French mustard, tomato sauce or grated horseradish. N.B. Salt beef is never used – it would make the *bouillon* undrinkable.

A *marmite*, by the way, is a cooking pot taller than it is wide; the small evaporation area enables it to be left simmering for a long period with minimum loss of liquid.

Clear soup and cold jelly

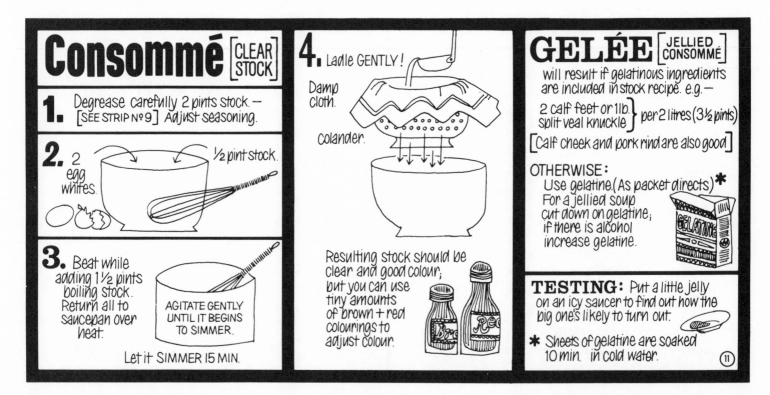

Consommé [CLEAR STOCK]

1. Degrease carefully 2 pints stock. — [SEE STRIP Nº 9] Adjust seasoning.

2. 2 egg whites. ½ pint stock.

3. Beat while adding 1½ pints boiling stock. Return all to saucepan over heat.

AGITATE GENTLY UNTIL IT BEGINS TO SIMMER.

Let it SIMMER 15 MIN.

4. Ladle GENTLY!

Damp cloth.

colander.

Resulting stock should be clear and good colour; but you can use tiny amounts of brown + red colourings to adjust colour.

GELÉE [JELLIED CONSOMMÉ]

will result if gelatinous ingredients are included in stock recipe. e.g. —

2 calf feet or 1lb. split veal knuckle } per 2 litres (3½ pints)

[Calf cheek and pork rind are also good]

OTHERWISE:
Use gelatine. (As packet directs)✱ For a jellied soup cut down on gelatine; if there is alcohol increase gelatine.

GELATINE

TESTING: Put a little jelly on an icy saucer to find out how the big one's likely to turn out.

✱ Sheets of gelatine are soaked 10 min. in cold water.

⑪

In the same way that *bouillon* (liquid from *pot-au-feu*) is a super version of *fonds brun*, so *consommé* is the next step up from *bouillon*.* Larousse says that *consommé* is 'meat stock that has been concentrated, clarified, and enriched'. The result must be clear and sparkling. All your equipment must be free from grease or dirt and you must have a light hand when dealing with the egg-whites so that they act as a magnet for all the particles in the stock. Some cooks also add $\frac{1}{2}$ lb. ground beef at the same time. Proceed as Strip. If the *consommé* is to be served cold then add a little extra salt for, like all cold foods, it needs extra flavouring. If it is served hot it should have a pea-sized piece of butter dropped into the pot so that it has what the French call 'eyes'. A glass of Madeira, port, brandy, or sherry is a popular addition a few minutes before serving. Mixed (cooked) *julienne* vegetables (page 114) are often used to garnish *consommé*; here are some other ideas. Sprinkle tapioca (1 oz. per pint) into *consommé*, simmer 15 minutes. Serve. Do exactly the same thing with pearl barley or sago. This is called *consommé aux perles du Japon*. Tiny *profiteroles* can be added to the soup as it's brought to the table. A *consommé célestine* has a *crêpe* cut into fine strips added to the *consommé*. Cooked rice can be used as a garnish. Any of the tiny decorative pastas are well suited to the garnishing of *consommés*. Make no mistake: any sort of *consommé* is a very expensive thing to manufacture. It's a luxury dish and should only be served to guests who will appreciate it. There is nothing more devastating than to have someone ask what brand of canned *consommé* you are using after you've broken your neck to produce this cornerstone of French *cuisine*.

*Some academic cookery experts use the old name '*consommé blanc*' to describe a *bouillon* and so have to call a *consommé* a 'double *consommé*' but these terms are rare and growing rarer.

Jelly for glazing and a base to go under it

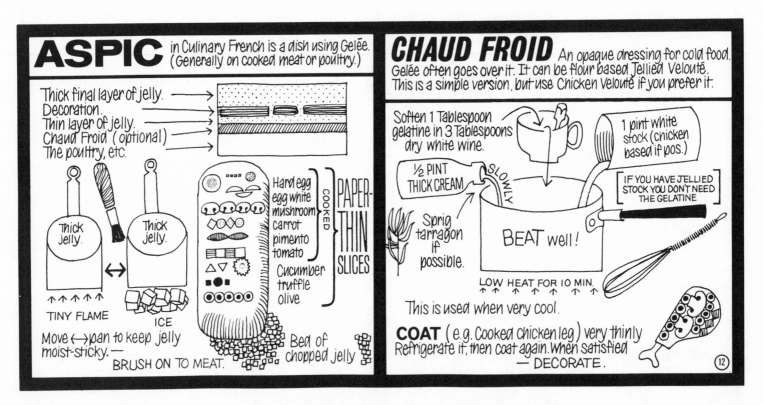

ASPIC in Culinary French is a dish using Gelée. (Generally on cooked meat or poultry.)

Thick final layer of jelly.
Decoration.
Thin layer of jelly.
Chaud Froid (optional)
The poultry, etc.

Thick jelly. ←→ Thick jelly.

TINY FLAME   ICE

Move ←→ pan to keep jelly moist-sticky. —

BRUSH ON TO MEAT.

Hard egg
egg white
mushroom
carrot
pimento
tomato
} COOKED

Cucumber
truffle
olive

PAPER-THIN SLICES

Bed of chopped jelly

CHAUD FROID An opaque dressing for cold food. Gelée often goes over it. It can be flour based Jellied Velouté. This is a simple version, but use Chicken Velouté if you prefer it.

Soften 1 Tablespoon gelatine in 3 Tablespoons dry white wine.

½ PINT THICK CREAM   SLOWLY

1 pint white stock (chicken based if pos.)

IF YOU HAVE JELLIED STOCK YOU DON'T NEED THE GELATINE

Sprig tarragon if possible.

BEAT well!

LOW HEAT FOR 10 MIN.

This is used when very cool.

COAT (e.g. Cooked chicken leg) very thinly
Refrigerate it, then coat again. When satisfied
— DECORATE.

⑫

This Strip just points the way to the whole wide world of cold dishes that the French chef calls *aspics*. They can be as simple as *œuf en gelée*, which is a cold *œuf mollet* (see page 158) put into a cup which has a thick layer of well-set jelly in it. More almost set jelly is poured until the egg is covered; then, when the jelly is set, the dish is unmoulded. Or an *aspic* can be a complex *chaud-froid de volaille*, which is a chicken poached (in stock if possible). I cut the chicken up before poaching it, but everyone else poaches them whole, then cuts the chicken up. The skin must be removed, the joints are covered with *chaud-froid* and decorated. When it's quite cold the aspic is added. The separate pieces of garnished chicken are placed upon a bed of chopped jelly or cold rice.

Poulet à la gelée is a different dish, for the chicken is first roasted and is not skinned. The cold roast chicken is cut into neat joints then reassembled, sticking the pieces together with aspic. Now the chicken is put into the closest-fitting dish possible. The chicken must be placed upside-down, then the dish is filled with almost set jelly. When it is set firm the bird is unmoulded and the rich colour of the roasted chicken is seen through the clear aspic.

Chaud-froid is not, as a rule, used on roasted items.

Of course aspics can be based upon many things other than poultry. A whole fish can be decorated and then painted with jelly; slices of *pâté*, ham or even bacon can be garnished. Those metal cones they sell in kitchenware shops – they are about the size of ice-cream cones – are for making ham cornets. The layer of ham is placed inside the metal cone, then a mixture of *pâté*, butter, *béchamel*, and 'chopped ham and chicken is pushed into it. The ham is pulled gently out and the whole thing coated with aspic. Serve on a bed of cress or rice.

Great sauces based on butter and egg

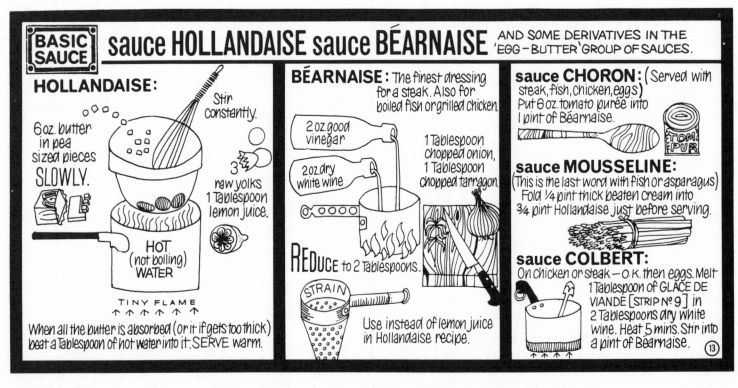

BASIC SAUCE sauce HOLLANDAISE sauce BÉARNAISE AND SOME DERIVATIVES IN THE 'EGG – BUTTER' GROUP OF SAUCES.

HOLLANDAISE:

6 oz. butter in pea sized pieces SLOWLY.

Stir constantly.

3 raw yolks 1 Tablespoon lemon juice.

HOT (not boiling) WATER

TINY FLAME

When all the butter is absorbed (or if it gets too thick) beat a Tablespoon of hot water into it. SERVE warm.

BÉARNAISE: The finest dressing for a steak. Also for boiled fish or grilled chicken.

2 oz. good vinegar

2 oz. dry white wine

1 Tablespoon chopped onion, 1 Tablespoon chopped tarragon.

REDUCE to 2 Tablespoons.

STRAIN

Use instead of lemon juice in Hollandaise recipe.

sauce CHORON: (Served with steak, fish, chicken, eggs) Put 6 oz. tomato purée into 1 pint of Béarnaise.

TOM. PUR

sauce MOUSSELINE: (This is the last word with fish or asparagus) Fold ¼ pint thick beaten cream into ¾ pint Hollandaise just before serving.

sauce COLBERT: On chicken or steak – o.k. then eggs. Melt 1 Tablespoon of GLACE DE VIANDE [STRIP N° 9] in 2 Tablespoons dry white wine. Heat 5 mins. Stir into a pint of Béarnaise. ⑬

For some strange reason these two sauces are always regarded with awe by those who have not tried making them. Yet *hollandaise* is a useful and simple garnish even if it is a little extravagant with butter. The butter is the heart of this operation. Three raw yolks will absorb the 6 oz. I have shown here without trouble, but the professional chef would add at least another 2 oz. of butter. At this stage, though, the absorbency power is waning and the task becomes difficult. If you have a blender you can slowly pour warm butter into the yolks and lemon juice. This is not a true *hollandaise* because you are relying upon the heat of the butter to 'cook' the egg yolk, but it will be quite good enough if you are in a hurry. Just to be on the safe side, put only 5 oz. of butter into it if you are using a blender. And warm the blender first.

Should you find that the sauce doesn't thicken, put one teaspoon of hot water and one tablespoon of failed sauce into a clean basin and add the sauce slowly drip by drip. A *hollandaise* that is to be served with fish may be based upon a concentrated fish *fumet* instead of lemon juice; that's particularly good with cutlets of salmon. *Hollandaise* is suitable for other sorts of fish cutlets (e.g. cod) or for luxury vegetables like tiny brussels sprouts, tiny green beans, asparagus, or cauliflower. *Mousseline* is a classic sauce for asparagus but will do for any of the items just mentioned. *Sauce maltaise* is a *hollandaise* that has had the juice of one orange mixed into it. The thinnest possible skin of two oranges is blanched for 2 mins., then finely chopped and also added. This is also a classic accompaniment for asparagus but can also be served with fried fish (plaice or sole) or with fried *scampi*.

All these sauces can be kept warm in a *bain-marie* for an hour before serving. And all of them are superb served cold e.g. cold *béarnaise* with cold beef.

A *beurre blanc* is, in effect, a *béarnaise* with the egg omitted. For the recipe see page 102. Served cold (e.g. with cold salmon) it is superior to any mayonnaise.

Sauce based on egg and oil

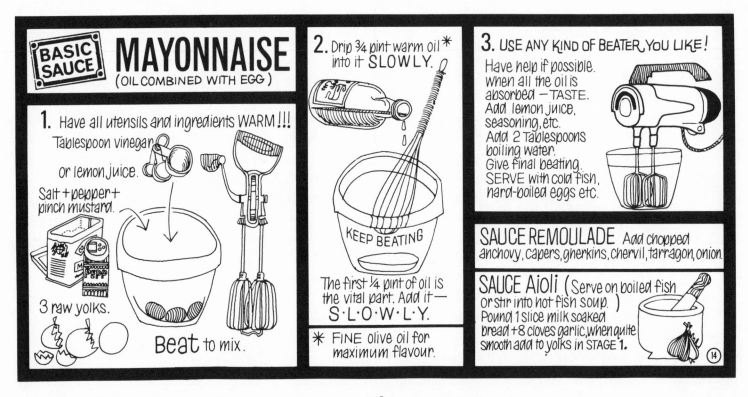

BASIC SAUCE **MAYONNAISE** (OIL COMBINED WITH EGG)

1. Have all utensils and ingredients WARM !!!
Tablespoon vinegar
or lemon juice.
Salt + pepper + pinch mustard.
3 raw yolks.
Beat to mix.

2. Drip ¾ pint warm oil* into it SLOWLY.
KEEP BEATING
The first ¼ pint of oil is the vital part. Add it— S·L·O·W·L·Y.
* FINE olive oil for maximum flavour.

3. USE ANY KIND OF BEATER, YOU LIKE!
Have help if possible. When all the oil is absorbed —TASTE. Add lemon juice, seasoning, etc. Add 2 Tablespoons boiling water. Give final beating. SERVE with cold fish, hard-boiled eggs etc.

SAUCE REMOULADE Add chopped anchovy, capers, gherkins, chervil, tarragon, onion.

SAUCE Aioli (Serve on boiled fish or stir into hot fish soup.) Pound 1 slice milk soaked bread + 8 cloves garlic, when quite smooth add to yolks in STAGE 1.

⑭

There are three common mistakes in making mayonnaise. One, adding too much oil at the start. So beat for a minute or so before beginning to add the oil, then do so very slowly. Two, using too much oil. Although experts may be able to get 5 ounces of oil into each egg yolk, I suggest you keep to my amounts for the first few times at least. Three, using oil or utensils that are too cold. Warm the mixing bowl and oil very slightly before you begin. After the first $\frac{1}{4}$ pint the dripping oil can become a trickle. Mayonnaise can be stored for a short period, but don't put it into a refrigerator or it might separate.

Sauce tartare is a mayonnaise variation served with fried or grilled fish. To make it, start with two hard-boiled egg yolks and mix very thoroughly with one raw egg yolk. Add seasoning and oil as described for mayonnaise. When the sauce is complete, add finely chopped tarragon, capers, gherkins, and parsley. Some cooks add the finely chopped hard egg whites too.

Sauce verte is another mayonnaise variation. To make it, blanch some chervil, tarragon, spinach, and watercress for about five minutes. Dry, then pound the green leaves thoroughly, finally pressing them through a sieve (a Mouli is useful here). This green purée is used to colour the mayonnaise. Some cooks add anchovy fillets to the greenery before pounding it, and this is equally correct.

Mayonnaise is very simple to make in a blender, but the high-speed blades aerate the mayonnaise and it becomes very light in colour. Hand-stirred mayonnaise is easily recognized from the commercial brands because of its dark golden colour.

Oil and vinegar dressing for cold foods

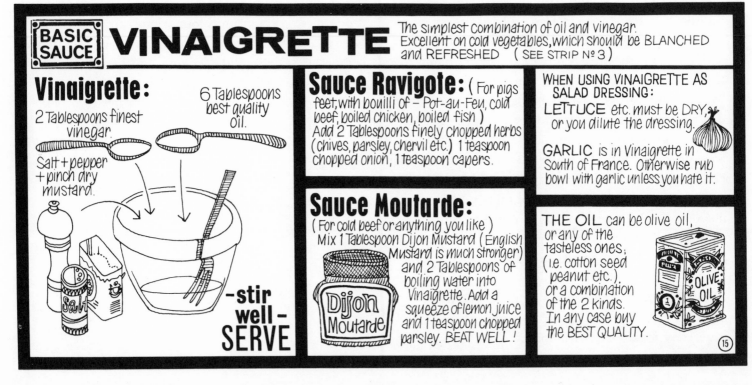

BASIC SAUCE

VINAIGRETTE

The simplest combination of oil and vinegar. Excellent on cold vegetables, which should be BLANCHED and REFRESHED (SEE STRIP N° 3)

Vinaigrette:

2 Tablespoons finest vinegar.

Salt + pepper + pinch dry mustard.

6 Tablespoons best quality oil.

–stir well– SERVE

Sauce Ravigote: (For pigs feet, with bouilli of – Pot-au-Feu, cold beef, boiled chicken, boiled fish)
Add 2 Tablespoons finely chopped herbs (chives, parsley, chervil etc.) 1 teaspoon chopped onion, 1 teaspoon capers.

Sauce Moutarde:
(For cold beef or anything you like)
Mix 1 Tablespoon Dijon Mustard (English Mustard is much stronger) and 2 Tablespoons of boiling water into Vinaigrette. Add a squeeze of lemon juice and 1 teaspoon chopped parsley. BEAT WELL !

Dijon Moutarde

WHEN USING VINAIGRETTE AS SALAD DRESSING:
LETTUCE etc. must be DRY, or you dilute the dressing.

GARLIC is in Vinaigrette in South of France. Otherwise rub bowl with garlic unless you hate it.

THE OIL can be olive oil, or any of the tasteless ones; (i.e. cotton seed peanut etc.), or a combination of the 2 kinds. In any case buy the BEST QUALITY.

OLIVE OIL

Vinaigrette is the simplest of dressings. Because of this its flavour is at the mercy of the quality of olive oil used. That wonderful *vinaigrette* dressing that you encountered in France is the same mixture with first-quality oil. Don't use an electric mixer or it will probably emulsify the mixture and the result will be a sort of ruined mayonnaise. There are plenty of additions to the dressing if you are looking round for some, but in the northern half of France it is unusual to find even garlic in it except for the restaurants where tourists expect it. The cook who wants something different can serve a cold *ravigote* sauce (see Strip) which is particularly good with cold vegetables, e.g. cauliflower, asparagus, cabbage even.

In England the *vinaigrette* dressing usually has lots of vinegar and little oil. Only too often this is because the oil has a flavour the cook doesn't like. So we are back with the oil again: buy only the very best, e.g. a Virgin oil from Provence. Wine merchants usually stock the finest oil, sometimes vinegar too.

American cooks add half a dozen more garnishes to the salad dressing, including lemon peel, chopped cheese, curry powder, ketchup, and, even more terrible, sugar. I give you this information to demon- strate the depths of depravity to which it is possible to sink. If you add any of those things, please cease to use the words *vinaigrette* dressing when you speak of it.

If you prefer to put oil and vinegar in separate bottles on the dining table so that guests may add it themselves, remember that the vinegar should go on the salad first, then the oil. If the oil goes on first it makes a coating upon which the vinegar can't obtain a grip. *Vinaigrette* should only touch lettuce at the last possible moment. On shredded cabbage it can go a little earlier, on tomato it can have up to an hour. Tomato salad reacts well with the cold *ravigote* sauce I have described above.

Easy steps to a perfect omelette

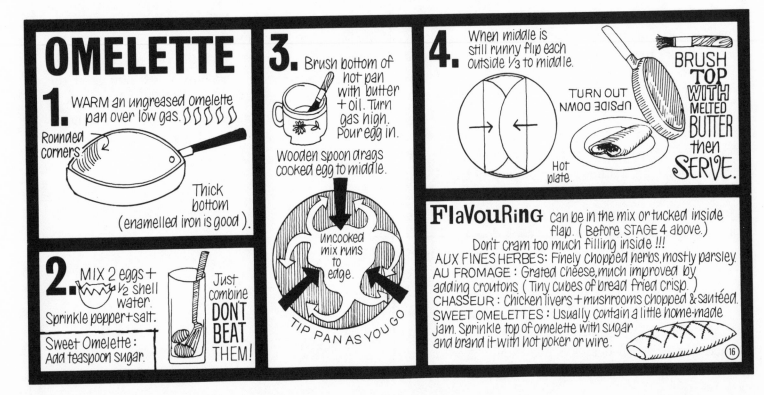

OMELETTE

1. WARM an ungreased omelette pan over low gas. Rounded corners. Thick bottom (enamelled iron is good).

2. MIX 2 eggs + ½ shell water. Sprinkle pepper + salt. Just combine DON'T BEAT THEM!

Sweet Omelette: Add teaspoon sugar.

3. Brush bottom of hot pan with butter + oil. Turn gas high. Pour egg in.

Wooden spoon drags cooked egg to middle.

Uncooked mix runs to edge. TIP PAN AS YOU GO

4. When middle is still runny flip each outside ⅓ to middle.

TURN OUT UPSIDE DOWN. Hot plate.

BRUSH TOP WITH MELTED BUTTER then SERVE.

FlaVouRing can be in the mix or tucked inside flap. (Before STAGE 4 above.) Don't cram too much filling inside !!!

AUX FINES HERBES: Finely chopped herbs, mostly parsley.

AU FROMAGE : Grated cheese, much improved by adding croutons (Tiny cubes of bread fried crisp.)

CHASSEUR : Chicken livers + mushrooms chopped & sautéed.

SWEET OMELETTES : Usually contain a little home-made jam. Sprinkle top of omelette with sugar and brand it with hot poker or wire.

In France they have a rather revolting description for a perfect omelette – they call it an *omelette baveuse* which means a 'dribbling omelette'. I only give this information to remind you that the centre must be undercooked. Once the omelette is closed and put on to a hot plate the centre will still be taking heat from its surround. It will be cooking. The centre must be quite runny when it's folded in order to get it to the table still moist.

The reason the third and fourth omelettes are usually a greater success than the first one is because the pan has had a chance to become thoroughly heated, so warm it well before you start. The pan must be clean, but cleaned with paper (newspaper will do); washing ruins the surface. Enamelled pans work well because the surface is slippery and gives the fat a chance to get under the egg-mix. Special non-stick surfaces are O.K., but the pan must be a heavy one.

Cheese has always been the basis of omelette recipes because it's such a quick, high-protein dish. Cooked chopped onion mixed with cheese and cold cooked potato is a popular French country-style omelette. Cheese and smoked haddock is an English idea. Sometimes the filling is just tiny pieces of bread fried crisp. In even poorer families they soak breadcrumbs in enough milk to moisten them and add one beaten egg and salt and pepper. This not only makes an egg into an omelette but also has a pleasant simple texture that is a change from a normal omelette. This is called a bread omelette. Try it.

Short pastry

PÂTE BRISÉE

A general purpose short pastry.

1. Utensils and ingredients must be cool !

Squeeze lemon. egg (optional) ¼ lb butter ¼ lb lard

4 tablespoons Castor Sugar for sweet pastry — Pâte Brisée Sucrée.

1 lb. Flour

For a tougher texture (e.g. certain pastry cases) use 2 eggs, omit lard.

2. Use finger TIPS.

Rub fat SMALLER & SMALLER like breadcrumbs.
Keep it cool — DON'T RUSH IT !

3. SPRINKLE a little water in —
tiniest pieces still sitting around.
NO sign of moisture
DOUGH JUST RIGHT
ROLL IT OUT
BEWARE: Too much water will wreck it !

4. If you want a pastry case : Roll out on floured board.
Any dry beans. tinfoil
DON'T STRETCH PASTRY ←⅛"+
THEN: Line 12" tin with pastry. Prick it.

5. Bake Reg 6 (400°F) for 8 mins. Remove foil and beans. Bake for another 2 or 3 mins.
Judge whether it's ready —
i.e. Is it going into oven again with raw filling ?
If not — fully cook it.
USE IT ! ⑰

The most difficult thing to explain in a cookery book is the amount of moisture that should be added to flour mixtures. Batter mixtures are like cream; they can be poured. A cake mixture is wet and will almost pour; it will drop from a spoon. Yeast mixtures are moist and plastic like modelling clay.

Pastry is always as dry as possible. Add the moisture sparsely, help the mixture to cling together by gentle light pressure. This is especially important if you use plain flour. Using self-raising flour makes the job easier but will give a different texture. French cooks are keen on *fraisage*, which is a pummelling or kneading of the dough before it's rolled. They would also leave the 'breadcrumbs' as large as tiny peas. If something is going wrong with your pastry it's certain to be due to too much water or overcooking. Coolness is important too and refrigeration before the final rolling out will make the particles of air expand more when it's cooked. In France the pastry would probably be left several hours before use. During this time the flour absorbs the fat particles, and the pastry loses its springy quality and becomes more manageable. Anything that smacks of ritual tends to overawe apprentices, and for this reason the professionals sometimes put on an act with all sorts of mumbo-jumbo, but when they are in a hurry the same cooks put it together like lightning. Strange to say the quality remains just as good. So make pastry as you would cook something you have done many times before, neither hurrying nor dawdling but giving it the amount of attention it needs and no more.

The final rolling out of the pastry is an important part of the process. Always roll the pastry to a consistent thickness. A texture that is wonderful rolled an eighth of an inch thick is terrible perhaps when thicker, and vice-versa. It's also important to roll the pastry to an even thickness, for uneven pastry will rise unevenly and where it is very thin will scorch.

. . . and making fruit tart the professional way

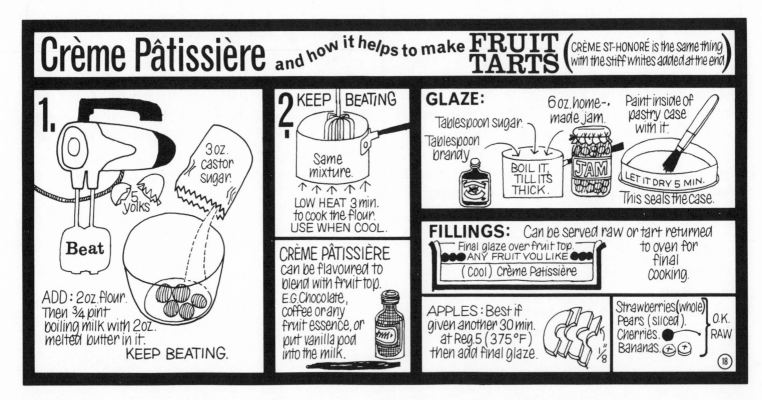

Crème Pâtissière *and how it helps to make* FRUIT TARTS
(CRÈME ST-HONORÉ is the same thing with the stiff whites added at the end)

1. Beat

5 yolks
3 oz. castor sugar.

ADD: 2 oz. flour. Then ¾ pint boiling milk with 2 oz. melted butter in it.
KEEP BEATING.

2. KEEP BEATING
Same mixture.
LOW HEAT 3 min. to cook the flour. USE WHEN COOL.

CRÈME PÂTISSIÈRE can be flavoured to blend with fruit top. E.G. Chocolate, coffee or any fruit essence, or put vanilla pod into the milk.

GLAZE:
Tablespoon sugar.
Tablespoon brandy
6 oz. home-made jam.
JAM
BOIL IT, TILL ITS THICK.
Paint inside of pastry case with it.
LET IT DRY 5 MIN.
This seals the case.

FILLINGS: Can be served raw or tart returned to oven for final cooking.
Final glaze over fruit top.
ANY FRUIT YOU LIKE
(Cool) Crème Pâtissière

APPLES: Best if given another 30 min. at Reg.5 (375°F) then add final glaze. 1"/8

Strawberries (whole) Pears (sliced). Cherries. Bananas. — O.K. RAW

(18)

Crème pâtissière or confectioner's custard is a filling for small or large *gâteaux* as well as being a base for the fruit in a fruit tart. The stirring is of immense importance and in a restaurant some apprentice will continue to stir it until the mixture is quite cool so that no skin forms on it. The result should be a thick, smooth cream with the flour well cooked (so it leaves no floury taste), and it will keep in a refrigerator for about a week.

A *crème St Honoré* is a variation on the *crème pâtissière*. To make this, proceed as in the Strip but beat the five egg whites until they are stiff, then fold them into the hot mixture after the flour is cooked at stage two. This is a popular filling for tarts and cream puffs. *Plombières* also use *crème St Honoré*. Dip sponge fingers into rum, coffee, or anything you fancy, arrange in a dish, then cover with a thin layer of suitable fruit. Top the dish with a generous layer of *crème St Honoré*. It must be very well chilled before serving (four hours at very least). There are thousands of *plombières* variations, e.g. mixing crushed macaroon into the cream or using ice-cream as one layer. *Crème St Honoré* can have flavours added to it: rum, brandy, cocoa, coffee, or various liqueurs. Some cooks add a trace of gelatine when it's cooling. Dissolve it first, of course. This might be necessary if you need the cream to be especially firm in a built-up confection.

Making *crème pâtissière* was the very first job I learned in a restaurant if you don't count sweeping the floor and getting beer for the chefs. It seemed a good idea at the time. It raised the level of the fruit and prevented it from making the pastry soggy. The finished tart looked as though it was just bursting with filling. The flaw was that once it was cut you saw that the fruit was just a thin layer at the top. Therefore when I made one for the kitchen staff it had a minimum of cream and a maximum of fruit. I still make them that way.

Savoury tart fillings which can be served alone

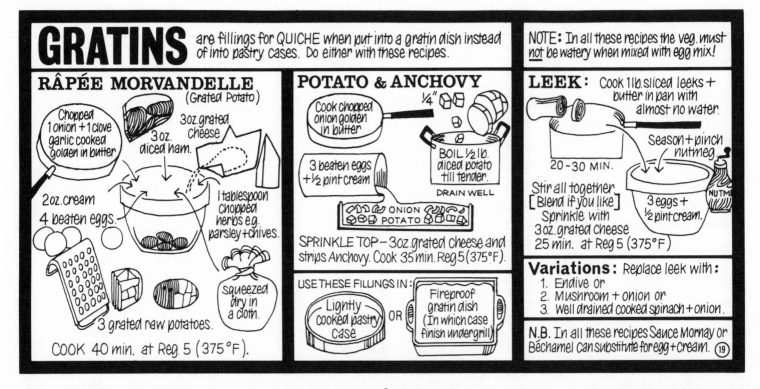

GRATINS are fillings for QUICHE when put into a gratin dish instead of into pastry cases. Do either with these recipes.

RÂPÉE MORVANDELLE
(Grated Potato)

Chopped 1 onion + 1 clove garlic cooked golden in butter

3oz. grated cheese

3oz. diced ham.

2oz. cream
4 beaten eggs.

1 tablespoon chopped herbs e.g. parsley + chives.

squeezed dry in a cloth.

3 grated raw potatoes.

COOK 40 min. at Reg. 5 (375°F).

POTATO & ANCHOVY

Cook chopped onion golden in butter

¼"

3 beaten eggs + ½ pint cream

BOIL ½ lb. diced potato till tender.

DRAIN WELL

ONION POTATO

SPRINKLE TOP – 3oz. grated cheese and strips Anchovy. Cook 35 min. Reg 5 (375°F).

USE THESE FILLINGS IN:

Lightly cooked pastry case

OR

Fireproof gratin dish (In which case finish under grill)

NOTE: In all these recipes the veg. must not be watery when mixed with egg mix!

LEEK:
Cook 1 lb. sliced leeks + butter in pan with almost no water.

20-30 MIN.

Season + pinch nutmeg.

Stir all together [Blend if you like] Sprinkle with 3oz. grated cheese 25 min. at Reg 5 (375°F)

3 eggs + ½ pint cream.

NUTME

Variations: Replace leek with:
1. Endive or
2. Mushroom + onion or
3. Well drained cooked spinach + onion.

N.B. In all these recipes Sauce Mornay or Béchamel can substitute for egg + cream. (19)

Someone said 'a *quiche* is anything plus a beaten egg' but in fact there are *quiche* recipes that don't have an egg in them. Although there are classic *quiche* and *gratin* recipes they do give you a chance to experiment. Left-over chicken, ham, or brains can be used and vegetables can be cut to a minimum. You can replace the cream and egg with a *sauce béchamel* or a *sauce mornay* as an economy measure, but it loses a lot of its quality. If you prefer it, make small individual *quiches* in tart tins. Most of these recipes are equally good hot or cold. *Quiche* and a bottle of wine make a typical French picnic lunch.

Gratin is a word that describes a coating that can be browned under a grill; *gratins* can be finished that way to get a crispy brown top, but if you do this with a *quiche* you must be careful not to scorch the pastry. Breadcrumbs sprinkled with melted butter, and used to cover a *gratin* before grilling it, will give a nice crusty look. A *gratin* can be prepared a little while in advance, but a *quiche* should not be assembled until just before you cook it, although the pastry case and filling can be prepared separately beforehand. An approximate measure when you are doing this is that an eight-inch pastry shell will hold one English pint of filling. Allow thirty fluid ounces for an eleven-inch pastry shell.

Olive, tomato, and anchovy is a favourite but because it's so important not to have a watery filling, the soft inside of the tomato is not used. The most famous *quiche* is *quiche Lorraine*. Blanch some thin slices of streaky bacon, then fry them in butter. Line the pastry case with them, fill with 3 beaten eggs plus half a pint of cream. Cook for 35 mins. at 375° F., Regulo 5. Some cooks add Gruyère or soft cream cheese under the bacon; do so if you wish. I personally always use ham in thick chunks when I make *quiche Lorraine*; this is slightly incorrect but I don't care.

Easy steps to a perfect soufflé

The SOUFFLE

1. 1½ OZ. FLOUR — 1½ oz. butter.

COOK 3 min.

GENTLE HEAT

Stir in 12oz. milk to make a creamy sauce.

Remove from heat.

Stir in 4 beaten yolks.

2. BEAT 5 egg whites stiff.

3. Fold whites + the sauce + 3 oz grated cheese together

GENTLY does it !!

4. 5½"

Tip in a buttered dish [Fr. Charlotte]

Sprinkle with cheese Bake. Reg. 6 (400°F) 30 min.

SERVE

VariATiONs:

Make this recipe into your own versions by either:

1. Flavouring the milk (cocoa or instant coffee).

2. Substituting fish or meat stock for the milk.

3. The cheese can be replaced by pounded chicken, ham, salmon, drained cooked spinach, shrimp, brains or sweetbreads. Hazelnuts or candied fruit.

20

Soufflés can be sweet or savoury. They are usually based upon a purée which has been thickened with egg-yolks. Stiffly beaten egg-whites are folded into the purée, then the whole thing is baked. Anything which follows that pattern is a *soufflé*, although the purée can sometimes be a thick *béchamel* sauce. For instance, the purée might be a potato purée, in which case it should have plenty of seasoning and butter mixed into it. Grated nutmeg is good too.

There are many different theories about how cooked a *soufflé* should be. Some cooks like the centre to be as dry as a sponge, others feel that the centre should be a semi-liquid that makes a sauce for the dryer outer crust. Lapérouse, in Paris, serve their Grand Marnier *soufflé* with a very crisp top and very liquid centre. It is superb. The well-cooked ones in my opinion should be served with a sauce, or cream in the case of a sweet *soufflé*.

I'm sure I don't have to tell you that the egg-whites must be fresh and without even a speck of yolk in them or they will never beat stiff. In a French kitchen the egg-whites would be beaten in an un-lined copper bowl. It is said that the action of the copper upon the egg-whites helps in the process of beating them stiff. Other gimmicks for helping with the beating is to add a pinch of salt or, some say, a pinch of cream of tartar. When the whites are folded into the mixture it must be gently done because it is those tiny bubbles in the beaten egg-white which will expand as the air inside them heats, and thus the *soufflé* will rise. So you see why the bubbles must be intact and well mixed. The best method is to turn the purée and yolk mixture into the stiffly beaten egg-white; while still stirring it round, tip the whole thing into the *soufflé* dish. This ensures that there are plenty of bubbles near the bottom of the dish. The most vital thing is to have the purée mixture of the same consistency as the beaten egg-whites. Now, as long as the oven is preheated before you put the *soufflé* into it, I don't see how you can go wrong.

Hot-water pastry for éclairs etc. Potato dumplings

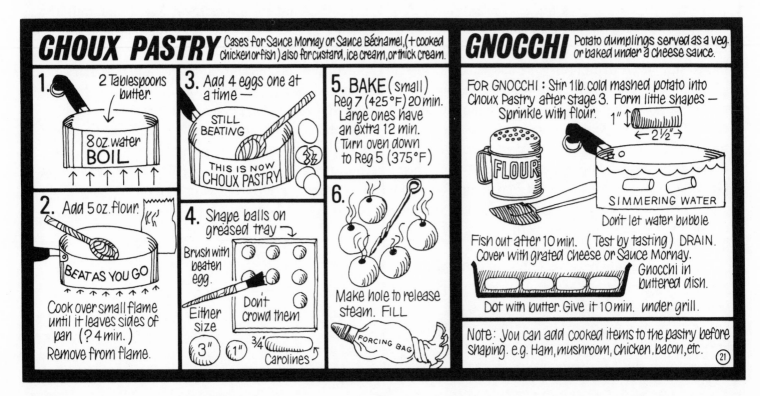

CHOUX PASTRY Cases for Sauce Mornay or Sauce Béchamel, (+ cooked chicken or fish) also for custard, ice cream, or thick cream.

1. 2 Tablespoons butter. 8 oz. water **BOIL**

2. Add 5 oz. flour. **BEAT AS YOU GO** Cook over small flame until it leaves sides of pan (? 4 min.) Remove from flame.

3. Add 4 eggs one at a time — STILL BEATING THIS IS NOW CHOUX PASTRY

4. Shape balls on greased tray. Brush with beaten egg. Don't crowd them. Either size. 3" 1" 3/4" Carolines

5. BAKE (small) Reg 7 (425°F) 20 min. Large ones have an extra 12 min. (Turn oven down to Reg 5 (375°F)

6. Make hole to release steam. FILL FORCING BAG

GNOCCHI Potato dumplings served as a veg. or baked under a cheese sauce.

FOR GNOCCHI : Stir 1 lb. cold mashed potato into Choux Pastry after stage 3. Form little shapes — Sprinkle with flour. 1" ← 2½" →

FLOUR SIMMERING WATER

Don't let water bubble

Fish out after 10 min. (Test by tasting) DRAIN. Cover with grated cheese or Sauce Mornay. Gnocchi in buttered dish.

Dot with butter. Give it 10 min. under grill.

Note: You can add cooked items to the pastry before shaping. e.g. Ham, mushroom, chicken, bacon, etc. ㉑

Choux pastry is the stuff of which éclairs are made. The cases are simple to make but they don't keep very well, in my experience, so make the quantity you intend to fill and use. If you fill the cases with *crème pâtissière*, thick cream, ice-cream, or custard, the cases can be lightly sprinkled with fine sugar and served but if you want something more complex the cases can be garnished. For instance, the cases can be painted with a glaze. The glaze can be melted jam or sugar and a drop of water heated to a sticky consistency. The glazed cases should then be rolled in chopped nuts (scorched nuts are best).

This same *choux* pastry can be dropped into deep fat for a minute or so. Keep the pieces of dough very small; they will swell up to about three times the size. Drain them well and sprinkle with fine sugar. Serve with coffee.

Gnocchi dishes are *gratins* like those on page 148 and can have garnishes of ham, bacon, etc. There are three different types of *gnocchi*. There's the one shown. There's one made from *choux* pastry without the addition of potato. It should have plenty of grated cheese stirred into it. The third type is made from semolina or *polenta* (a yellow maize flour). Cook the semolina in milk so that it goes to a stiff mixture, then add egg yolks (two per pint) and let it get cold. Cut the cold semolina pudding (that's what it is, although without sugar) into shapes and proceed as shown in the Strip; there is no need to poach them.

Gnocchi is usually served before the meat course as a pasta would be, but potato *gnocchi* can be served as a vegetable to accompany a simple meat dish.

Using meat or fish pieces to make an elegant meal

Quenelles are fluffy dumplings based upon raw meat or fish poached in stock.

1. PURÉE 1 lb. boneless RAW VEAL or RAW CHICKEN or RAW FISH e.g. Whiting, Cod (Fillets are easier)

Do it any way you like.

Twice thro' this

Blender

2. Make a **Panada** i.e. ½ lb soft breadcrumbs ½ pint milk

SOAK 20 min.

Then heat it until it leaves sides of pan.

3. Assemble: Panada — Purée. MIX WELL seasoning + nutmeg.

Then: 2 beaten eggs, 1 teaspoon at a time — slowly!

4. Wet spoons. FORM BETWEEN SPOONS

DROP into simmering stock.

ABOUT 20 MIN.

Salted water will do.

5. The same mixture can make a SAVOURY MOUSSE

buttered mould

WATER JACKET.

Dish mustn't rest on bottom.

BAKE at Reg 4 (350°F) until it shrinks from side of mould.

EITHER WAY serve with a sauce. e.g.—
Sauce Madère — (Strip N°10)
Sauce Choron
Sauce Colbert } (Strip N°13)

㉒

There is a theory that the word *quenelle* is based upon the old Anglo-Saxon word *knylle*, which meant to pound or grind. Whether it's true or not, this process is certainly the most important part of the preparation. *Quenelles* are a sort of fluffy dumpling made from any game, crustacean, meat, fish, or poultry. They come in all shapes and sizes and the largest are often decorated with truffles.

Quenelles are served with either a cream-type sauce (e.g. shrimp or mushroom) or just a *béchamel*. They can be served as a garnish in a soup or, to ascend into the realms of *haute cuisine*, they can be part of a garnish around a complex centre dish.

The consistency of the mixture is the part where it is most likely to go wrong, so try poaching one as an experiment, then change the mixture accordingly. For instance, if the cooked *quenelle* seems dry and heavy the mixture is too solid. If the cooked *quenelle* breaks up in the water the mixture is too light (be sure that the poaching liquid isn't bubbling for that's asking for trouble). The mixture should be rather like a *soufflé*, with just enough texture to hold its own shape without collapsing.

Some recipes like to mix creamed butter and/or cream into the mixture at stage three, which although it improves the flavour makes them a little more difficult to handle, in my opinion, but try that if you wish; 3 oz. of each is about right. Another refinement at stage three would be to sieve the mixture through a fine sieve. That isn't imperative, but if you have a blender the mixture will be improved by a whirl at this stage. If you shape the *quenelles* with spoons you should dip them into very hot water between each action. If you don't use the spoons you can either shape them by hand – into tiny sausages – on a floured board or pipe tiny ones (suitable for soup garnish) through a piping bag.

Cooked left-overs become a party centrepiece

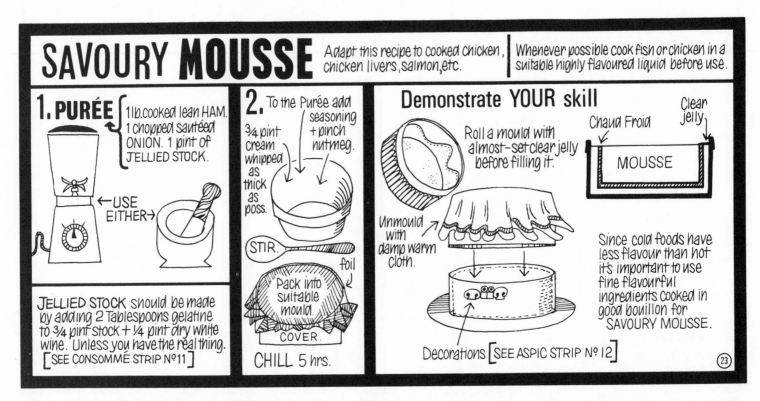

SAVOURY MOUSSE

Adapt this recipe to cooked chicken, chicken livers, salmon, etc.

Whenever possible cook fish or chicken in a suitable highly flavoured liquid before use.

1. PURÉE
1 lb. cooked lean HAM. 1 chopped sautéed ONION. 1 pint of JELLIED STOCK.

←USE EITHER→

JELLIED STOCK should be made by adding 2 Tablespoons gelatine to ¾ pint stock + ¼ pint dry white wine. Unless you have the real thing. [SEE CONSOMMÉ STRIP N° 11]

2.
To the Purée add seasoning + pinch nutmeg.

¾ pint cream whipped as thick as poss.

STIR.

Pack into suitable mould.

foil

COVER.

CHILL 5 hrs.

Demonstrate YOUR skill

Roll a mould with almost-set clear jelly before filling it.

Chaud Froid

Clear Jelly

MOUSSE

Unmould with damp warm cloth.

Since cold foods have less flavour than hot it's important to use fine flavourful ingredients cooked in good bouillon for SAVOURY MOUSSE.

Decorations [SEE ASPIC STRIP N° 12]

(23)

There are names used in French *cuisine* that have very special and exact meanings. *Mousse* is not one of these words. If you order a *mousse* you will possibly be served a hot dish with a hot sauce. Sometimes the *mousse* is stiffened by means of 2 egg-whites instead of with gelatine. In this case the *mousse* is cooked in a water jacket for about 30 minutes, then it's allowed to cool, but this is an exception to the rule. So is a chocolate *mousse*, which needs neither gelatine nor egg because the chocolate itself is a stiffening ingredient. This fact leads to all sorts of disasters in cookery for the cook who thinks of chocolate as only a flavouring, substitutes another flavour (e.g. coffee), and wonders why the thing flops.

Mousse can be translated as foam froth, the head on a glass of beer, or as cream. In French cooking it is usually defined as a sieved, pounded preparation bound with sauce or cream. Smaller ones with cream are called *mousseline*.

As a general rule all *mousses* can be thought of as creamy jellies containing ingredients that are either cooked or need no cooking (e.g. strawberries). *Mousses* can be made well in advance and are a chance for the cook to show off. Serve them glowing through a thick layer of beautifully clear jelly, decorated or plain, with or without a good white *chaud-froid* around the *mousse*. *Chaud-froid* is unnecessary if the *mousse* itself is a good colour and texture. Such a centrepiece will let you serve the simplest of following dishes without apology.

A fish *mousse* – smoked haddock or cod is fine – makes an excellent *entrée*. Served with a chilled sparkling wine it can make a memorable snack on a summer evening or – if you transport it carefully – it can be the centrepiece of a picnic.

A dozen roles for the egg

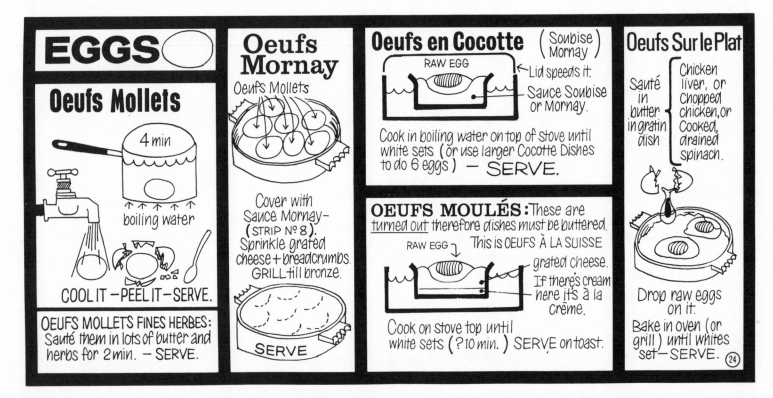

EGGS

Oeufs Mollets

4 min

boiling water

COOL IT — PEEL IT — SERVE.

OEUFS MOLLETS FINES HERBES: Sauté them in lots of butter and herbs for 2 min. — SERVE.

Oeufs Mornay

Oeufs Mollets

Cover with Sauce Mornay — (STRIP N° 8). Sprinkle grated cheese + breadcrumbs. GRILL till bronze.

SERVE

Oeufs en Cocotte (Soubise / Mornay)

RAW EGG

← Lid speeds it.
— Sauce Soubise or Mornay.

Cook in boiling water on top of stove until white sets (or use larger Cocotte Dishes to do 6 eggs) — SERVE.

OEUFS MOULÉS: These are turned out therefore dishes must be buttered.

RAW EGG   This is OEUFS À LA SUISSE

grated cheese.
If there's cream here it's à la crème.

Cook on stove top until white sets (?10 min.) SERVE on toast.

Oeufs Sur le Plat

Sauté in butter in gratin dish { Chicken liver, or Chopped chicken, or Cooked, drained spinach.

Drop raw eggs on it.
Bake in oven (or grill) until whites set — SERVE. (24)

The white of a new-laid egg clings to its yolk. When dropped into a pan, a mound of clear white forms a sharp hump over the yellow, the yolk itself is firm and not easy to break. I won't tell you what a stale egg is like, for you are handling those every day. The fresh egg is heavy, for the moisture inside has not had a chance·to evaporate through the porous shell.

Hard-boiled eggs – *œufs durs* – are put into plenty of fast-boiling water. Counting from the time the water recommences boiling, give the eggs eight minutes (for extra-large eggs make it ten minutes). Then put the eggs into a large bowl of cold water (if you only have a small bowl, run cold water into it) before shelling them.

When a French cook says *œufs frits* he means something a little different to the anglicized fried egg which corresponds more to sautéing than frying. For *œufs frits* drop a shelled egg into at least half an inch of very hot oil or fat. Using a wooden spoon, heap the white over the yolk so that the cooked egg will have a soft yolk entirely surrounded by crisp white. Drain on kitchen paper before serving.

Œufs pochés more than any other recipe demands new-laid eggs. Into a pint of boiling water put half an ounce of salt, and a tablespoon of vinegar. Stir the water, and into the 'eye' in the centre of the swirl drop the shelled eggs. Keep the water below boiling point. When the white is firm bring the egg out in a draining spoon. Dip it into warm water to remove the taste of the vinegar, then use kitchen paper to ensure it's quite dry. For appearance you can trim the edges of the white with kitchen scissors.

For a description of boiled and coddled eggs see page 16.

No end to the variations for pancakes

CRÊPES

1. BEAT until like cream.

½ pint milk *

8 OZ. FLOUR

Use any **BEATER** you like. A blender is perhaps the best

1 egg

3 Tablespoons melted butter.

SWEET ONES
(CRÊPES SUCRÉES)

1 Tablespoon castor sugar
2 Tablespoons brandy (or etc.)

* ¼ pint milk + ¼ pint water gives a lighter more fragile crêpe — try it.

2. HEAT heavy pan.

Brush with oil * + butter.

Pour mix in — tip to spread it even.
THEY MUST BE **THIN!**

PILE THEM UP

COOK BOTH SIDES

Saucepan of hot water

* Nut oil (not olive oil) for sweet ones.

FILL with anything from jam to caviar.
DOUSE them with anything from Aioli to Armagnac.

Gâteau de Crêpes

Pour sauce over it — or brandy and sugar

Sweet or savoury fillings
BAKE: Moderate oven.

Gratin de Crêpes

Sauce or etc. all over it.

Sweet or savoury fillings

BAKE: Moderate oven till brown.

25

There is an old Russian proverb that says 'the first pancake is always a lump'. It doesn't go on to explain why, and I'll suggest it's because the pan isn't hot enough and the mixture isn't at the right consistency, and perhaps the cook is a little too anxious. After the first few pancakes are made this has been remedied; they are coming off the production line like aspirins. Don't stop. Pancakes are a useful stand-by and will keep quite well. In Northern France not only will the *crêperie* sell you pancakes of various flours and with a wide range of fillings, but they will sell you a dozen cooked pancakes to take home for breakfast too. A favourite way to deal with cold pancakes at breakfast time is to spread them with butter, roll them up, and dunk them into hot coffee as you eat them. Try that and you'll understand why *croissants* haven't made much headway in Brittany.

Another recipe from the same region is *crêpes bonne femme*. Add grated orange peel and Calvados (rum will do) to the mixture. When cooked, put apple sauce inside and fold into quarters, sprinkle with chopped almonds. Serve.

Crêpes with stuffing of any kind are called *pannequets* in culinary French and the varieties are endless. They are one of the best ways of dealing with leftover cooked meats and poultry. Cooked *crêpe* can also be cut into strips or shapes and used as a garnish for *bouillon*. It's quite possible to get a good pancake using only 4 oz. flour, a large spoonful of baking powder, and mixing it with warm water. Many commercial mixes are made this way, using not even dried egg.

A luxury dish from the deep-fryer

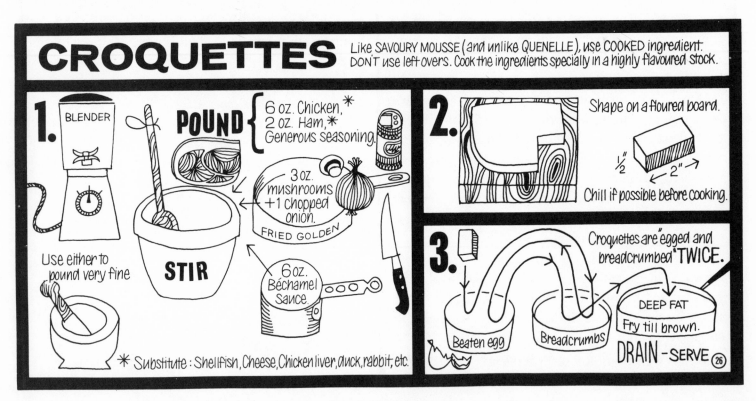

CROQUETTES Like SAVOURY MOUSSE (and unlike QUENELLE), use COOKED ingredient. DON'T use left overs. Cook the ingredients specially in a highly flavoured stock.

1. BLENDER

Use either to pound very fine

POUND { 6 oz. Chicken,* 2 oz. Ham,* Generous seasoning.

3 oz. mushrooms +1 chopped onion. FRIED GOLDEN

STIR

6 oz. Béchamel Sauce.

* Substitute: Shellfish, Cheese, Chicken liver, duck, rabbit, etc.

2. Shape on a floured board.

½" ← 2" →

Chill if possible before cooking.

3. Croquettes are "egged and breadcrumbed" TWICE.

Beaten egg   Breadcrumbs

DEEP FAT Fry till brown.

DRAIN - SERVE (26)

162

Croquettes are basically small preparations made in many different shapes; cylinders, cones, and balls. Ideally they are made from a superb, highly-flavoured filling cooked especially for them, rather than from left-overs. Croquettes are always coated twice for a very good reason; the inside of a good croquette is soft and creamy and unless coated twice would be very liable to burst during frying. Getting the croquettes very cold before cooking them will also keep them intact in the final process. Keep the fat clean – it's those small burnt flecks in it which cause the smoke and discoloured food – and drain the croquettes well. Serve them on a hot plate and if necessary keep them warm in the oven. Large croquettes are usual as a main dish while the tiny ones are best as an *hors d'œuvre*.

The perfect croquette is golden and appetizing in colour, crisp in outer texture and soft and creamy inside. Cress or parsley is a useful garnish. Sometimes rich sauces like *sauce madère* (page 130) are served too.

There are also sweet croquettes. Chestnut croquettes are made from crushed *marrons glacés* mixed with crushed macaroons which have been soaked in rum. This is dipped into egg as shown. So now you know the rules of the game, go ahead; there's no reason why you can't invent half a dozen new ones, before supper time.

Pork and cabbage make a hearty meal

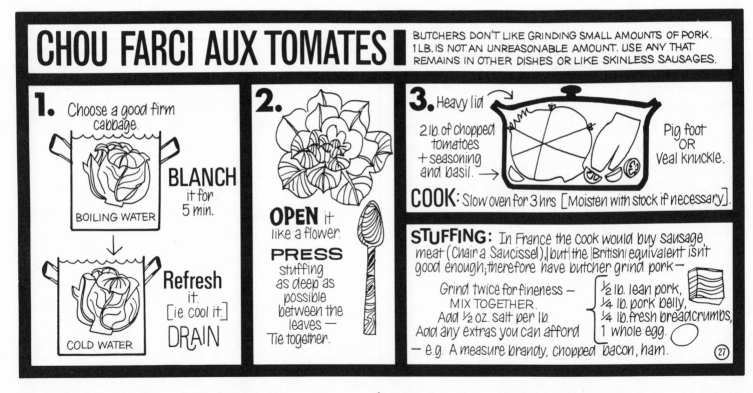

CHOU FARCI AUX TOMATES

BUTCHERS DON'T LIKE GRINDING SMALL AMOUNTS OF PORK. 1 LB. IS NOT AN UNREASONABLE AMOUNT. USE ANY THAT REMAINS IN OTHER DISHES OR LIKE SKINLESS SAUSAGES.

1. Choose a good firm cabbage.

BOILING WATER

BLANCH it for 5 min.

Refresh it. [ie. cool it.] **DRAIN**

COLD WATER

2. **OPEN** it like a flower. **PRESS** stuffing as deep as possible between the leaves — Tie together.

3. Heavy lid

2 lb. of chopped tomatoes + seasoning and basil. →

Pig foot OR Veal knuckle.

COOK: Slow oven for 3 hrs [Moisten with stock if necessary].

STUFFING: In France the cook would buy sausage meat (Chair a Saucissel), but the British equivalent isn't good enough; therefore have butcher grind pork —

Grind twice for fineness —
MIX TOGETHER.
Add ½ oz. salt per lb.
Add any extras you can afford
— e.g. A measure brandy, chopped bacon, ham.

½ lb. lean pork,
¼ lb. pork belly,
¼ lb. fresh breadcrumbs,
1 whole egg.

(27)

Like so many dishes of the world this is a way of making a cheap vegetable extend the use of meat. In French peasant cooking the less meat it was possible to get into the cabbage, the better, but for more sophisticated tables the cook might prefer to hollow out the centre of the cabbage in order to get a maximum amount of meat inside it.

A variation is to take the blanched cabbage to pieces and make the meat and cabbage into layers. A layer of pork belly to start it off, then a layer of cabbage leaves, then a thin layer of meat stuffing, etc. The tomatoes are optional.

Yet another way is to wrap the meat up into little parcels using one cabbage leaf each time. When cooked, serve the parcels carefully so they don't unwrap. Such parcels (especially if stuffed with pork) are delicious cold. Serve with *vinaigrette* if you like.

When the cabbage is used in layers, sauerkraut can be substituted. Tinned sauerkraut will do fine, but make sure that it is well drained and forked apart before using it. Salt pork (soak for an hour or so before cooking it) is a traditional accompaniment for sauerkraut (*choucroute*) and it is usual to cook them almost to a jam.

The dish developed by people who could afford nothing else is a casserole of cabbage and potato. The potato can, if you wish, be fried, and in any case use lots of good quality fat (meat dripping is best of all). Make layers of potato and fresh blanched cabbage, having first lined the dish with thin streaky rashers, as you would for a *terrine*. Put a trace of stock in before closing the rashers and the close-fitting lid. Such a casserole is nowadays best served with or after a meat course.

Cold jellied pork

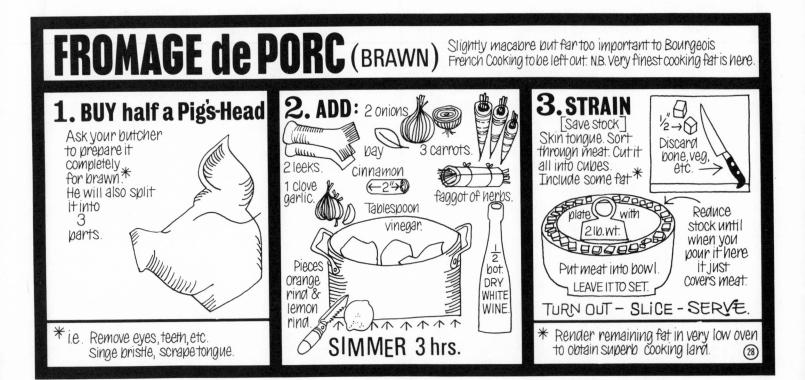

FROMAGE de PORC (BRAWN) Slightly macabre but far too important to Bourgeois French Cooking to be left out. N.B. Very finest cooking fat is here.

1. BUY half a Pig's-Head

Ask your butcher to prepare it completely* for brawn. He will also split it into 3 parts.

* i.e. Remove eyes, teeth, etc. Singe bristle, scrape tongue.

2. ADD: 2 onions

2 leeks. bay 3 carrots.
cinnamon
←—2"—→
1 clove garlic. faggot of herbs.
Tablespoon vinegar.

Pieces orange rind & lemon rind.

½ bot. DRY WHITE WINE.

SIMMER 3 hrs.

3. STRAIN

[Save stock]
Skin tongue. Sort through meat. Cut it all into cubes. Include some fat*

½" ⬜→⬜ Discard bone, veg, etc. →

plate with 2 lb. wt.

Reduce stock until when you pour it here it just covers meat.

Put meat into bowl. LEAVE IT TO SET.

TURN OUT – SLICE – SERVE.

* Render remaining fat in very low oven to obtain superb cooking lard. 28

Most *charcuteries* in France are sources of wonder to the ambitious cook. The care with which the *crêpinettes*, *boudin*, *galantine*, truffled *foie gras*, and rolled shoulders are prepared and garnished is a joy to see. Even now, when more and more items of *charcuterie* are made in large factories, it is still possible to find a little man around the corner, and in any case the manufactured items are several generations beyond anything yet available in your local shop in Britain.

The recipe shown here is sometimes called *fromage de tête* or *tête pressée* and it may contain pieces of heart or tongue. Sometimes luxury items, like truffle, or pistachio nuts, are added for flavour and colour.

The cheek has the best flavour. It can be served separately. Ask the butcher to score the skin. After soaking briefly, simmer it for 25 minutes per pound. Drain it, then grill it so that the skin becomes crackling. When served this is a fine cut of tender meat not unlike ham.

Fat from pig's head is the finest type of cooking lard. Meat from this region is the favourite ingredient for the manufacture of *rillettes* (page 118). N.B. In all these recipes it's important that the pig's head is fresh, not salted.

The finished brawn is unmoulded by using a warm damp towel around the bowl while holding it inverted. The brawn is sliced into as fine slices as you can make. Use it for *hors d'œuvres*, sandwiches, supper, or as a main dish on a summer's day. Next time you go into a *charcuterie* you'll be able to display a fine proprietorial manner.

France's most popular way with fish

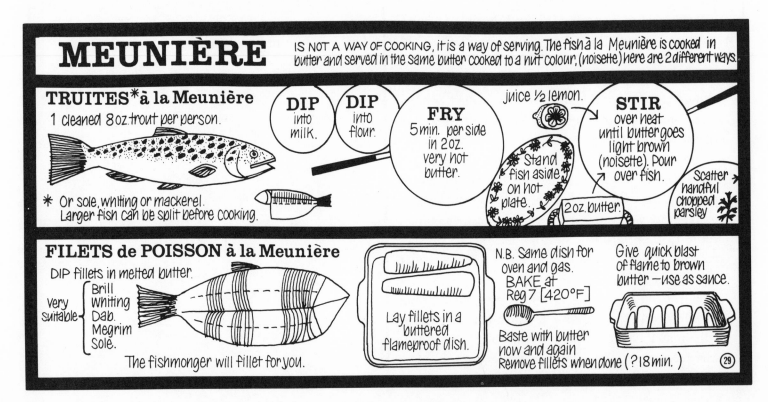

MEUNIÈRE IS NOT A WAY OF COOKING, it is a way of serving. The fish à la Meunière is cooked in butter and served in the same butter cooked to a nut colour, (noisette) here are 2 different ways.

TRUITES*à la Meunière

1 cleaned 8 oz. trout per person.

* Or sole, whiting or mackerel.
Larger fish can be split before cooking.

DIP into milk.

DIP into flour.

FRY 5 min. per side in 2 oz. very hot butter.

juice ½ lemon.

Stand fish aside on hot plate.

2 oz. butter.

STIR over heat until butter goes light brown (noisette). Pour over fish.

Scatter handful chopped parsley

FILETS de POISSON à la Meunière

DIP fillets in melted butter.

very suitable — Brill, Whiting, Dab, Megrim, Sole.

The fishmonger will fillet for you.

Lay fillets in a buttered flameproof dish.

N.B. Same dish for oven and gas. BAKE at Reg 7 [420°F]

Baste with butter now and again. Remove fillets when done (?18 min.)

Give quick blast of flame to brown butter — use as sauce.

This way of cooking would be called *sauté*, but to say *à la meunière* tells so much more about the preparation. We know at once that it's probably going to be a whole, small fish and we know too that it's going to be cooked in butter. A perfectionist might say that it indicates clarified butter (page 118). The fish when served will have a generous amount of butter served with it and that butter will probably be cooked to a nutty brown colour. It's a good bet in any decent restaurant that the plate will be a hot one because there is a moment of delay while the butter is scorched. What's more, you'd be right to expect that this is the plate that the waiter will give priority to, bringing it immediately from stoveside to table top.

So you see that this recipe has simple but rigid rules of behaviour. Everything must be done just right, no radish roses or cucumber lilies will save you if you leave the cooked fish to go soggy on an ice-cold plate. Slow cooking is another way of making the fish go soggy, but don't have the heat so high that you burn the skin of the fish. You'll need to have a good thick pan because even clarified butter will burn quite easily. And above all get it to the table while the butter is still a-bubble. An automatic cooker (a cooking pan with a heat control) will not only keep the butter at exactly the temperature you choose but it will do it at the table!

Truite amandine is exactly the same, but you add a big spoonful of blanched almonds to the butter, letting them brown in it. The whole thing is then tipped over the fish.

Cooking fish in a paper bag

Mackerel in Papillotes

USE THIS SAME METHOD FOR COOKING ANYTHING FROM VEAL CHOPS TO SHRIMPS.

1 small mackerel per person.

Have it split and boned.

Stuff with mixture.

Butter piece of greaseproof paper [Foil will do].

fold.

seal edges

BAKE: Reg 4 (355°F) 25-30 min.

SERVE in cases or out.

MIXTURE for fish OR invent your own.
{
Parsley
Capers
Butter
Lemon peel
Fennel
Crumbs
Salt & pepper.

Just salt, pepper and butter will do for meat or fish.

NOTE: Meat in Papillotes should be sautéed for a few min. first. Accompany meat with a spoonful of MIREPOIX (See Strip N°5).

30

Heavy lids, pie crusts, puddings, pastry seals, so many methods of cookery are devices to hold flavour inside a totally closed area. These *papillotes* work on the same principle. Ideally their contents should be raw and the envelopes not opened until the cooking is quite finished. There is a certain amount of judgement needed to time it, for there is no way of testing or observing how it's going. That's why they are usually cooked in a slow or moderate oven where a few minutes' error won't make too much difference.

As a rule meat cooked in a *papillote* is sautéd a little first. This is not to shorten the cooking process but to brown the meat for added flavour. This can also apply to onion if used as flavouring. Under no circumstances should cold, cooked ingredients be used for the *papillotes*. Raw beef shredded or in thin slices can be cooked this way, so can any other sort of meat or poultry.

The most usual filling remains fish. It can be a slice or a fillet of any sort of fish. Seasonings and flavourings are usually generously applied and a trickle of cream is not unusual. In medieval Europe ginger was a favourite flavouring for fish – probably because transport prevented the fish from arriving still fresh – and in Chinese cooking this is still a favourite garnish. Although it's not any sort of French recipe, let me suggest that a *papillote* is a good chance to reassemble that combination.

Pork stuffing for poultry or served as a terrine

FARCE This is a MEATY STUFFING. Use it to make a terrine as here or for any recipe requiring sausage meat.

1. ¾ lb. lean pork, ¾ lb. lean veal, ¾ lb. belly of pork.* } Ground up (Twice if you like smooth texture).

1 tot brandy

1 clove garlic (crushed).

Leave it to **marinade** overnight.

BIG glass DRY SHERRY (Dry wine will do).

1 chopped onion.

＊ In France they would use LARD GRAS (fat from loin).

2. ADD: [1 tsp. salt per lb. mix].

3 Tablespoons soft crumbs, thyme, 2 beaten eggs, pinch nutmeg.

STIR WELL USE IT!

3. Arrange **Decorations**

Ham fat.
Truffles.
Ham slice.
Pistachio nuts.
Rolled ham slices.

4. To make a **TERRINE**

Very thin bacon or thin sheets of pork fat.

Split calf's foot.

Cook in water jacket. Reg. 3 (335°F) for 2 hrs. Cool under 2 lb. weight. SERVE: Cold, sliced. (See Aspic Strip N°12 for décor ideas) ③

A *farce* is a forcemeat, which is the same thing as a stuffing. There are literally hundreds of them and even to list the groups and explain them would need more space than I have here. So I have done what I have done elsewhere in this book: concentrated upon the sort of knowledge that a cook in a small French country hotel would have.

The *farce* I have given here is a good standard one and there are others in this book, including the ones in the *quenelles* recipe (page 154). These meat mixtures can be varied according to what you need. More veal will add lightness and more pork adds flavour. Pig liver can be added if you want even more flavour. In my opinion a *terrine* made of about 60 per cent pig liver and 40 per cent pork fat is the best *terrine* of all. Pork fat (that from under the skin of the loin is best of all) will give added smoothness and will give a soft spreadable type of *terrine*. Added bread-crumbs will give firmness. The texture is controlled by how finely the mixture is minced. A typical country-style mixture might have pig liver, salt tongue, and hare, plus generous pork fat. The mixture is ground once, fairly coarsely.

A rabbit *terrine* will have chopped rabbit in it, perhaps not more than 25 per cent of the total. The same goes for any other type of *terrine*, e.g. hare, turkey, or pigeon. Such ingredients must, of course, be boned and added raw.

A *terrine*, incidentally, has exactly the same meat content as a *pâté*, but the latter has a pastry case. Any suitable forcemeat can be used as stuffing for poultry, although by putting the meat mixture inside, the roasting times are very much increased. It's better to cook the stuffing alongside.

Cold chicken can be a masterpiece

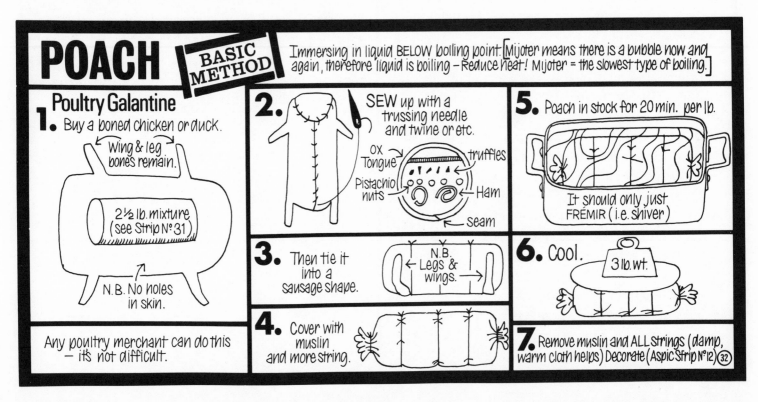

POACH — BASIC METHOD

Immersing in liquid BELOW boiling point. [Mijoter means there is a bubble now and again, therefore liquid is boiling – Reduce heat! Mijoter = the slowest type of boiling.]

Poultry Galantine

1. Buy a boned chicken or duck.

Wing & leg bones remain.

2½ lb. mixture (see Strip N° 31)

N.B. No holes in skin.

Any poultry merchant can do this – it's not difficult.

2. SEW up with a trussing needle and twine or etc.

OX Tongue — truffles
Pistachio nuts — Ham
seam

3. Then tie it into a sausage shape.

N.B. Legs & wings.

4. Cover with muslin and more string.

5. Poach in stock for 20 min. per lb.

It should only just FRÉMIR (i.e. shiver)

6. Cool.

3 lb. wt.

7. Remove muslin and ALL strings (damp, warm cloth helps) Decorate (Aspic Strip N° 12) ㉜

This cold stuffed chicken really wears the title *'galantine de volaille à la gelée'*. There is a very similar recipe in which the chicken is eaten while still hot. Such a dish is called a *ballotine*. These dishes depend very much upon the poaching or simmering process, i.e. keeping the temperature at a fixed point below the boiling point of water. A poached egg is cooked in exactly the same way. It is important that the water is deep and the chicken totally immersed in it, for if it is not surrounded with the heat of the water the cooking times will be altered. Many dishes cooked in water jackets on the stove-top go wrong because the water is not deep enough and so only the bottom part of the food is cooking. So be sure there is plenty of water; and the tin of water should be covered, if only with tin-foil, to keep the steam in. The bird should be turned every now and again to keep it cooking evenly.

While the bird is cooling the weight keeps the meat pressed together and removes the air pockets which have been there since you originally sewed it up. Those air pockets will make ugly slices that will break up when you are carving. So put the weight on – you'll have various packets of marked weights in the pantry – but don't make it too heavy or you'll squeeze the juices out of it.

The finished *galantine* will keep for about a week in a cold place. When it goes in the refrigerator wrap it well to prevent drying up. Ideally, though, the *galantine* is a dish made for a big party. Eat it while the 'oo's' and 'ahh's' are still echoing around the ceiling. It will never taste the same again.

All you need to know about chicken

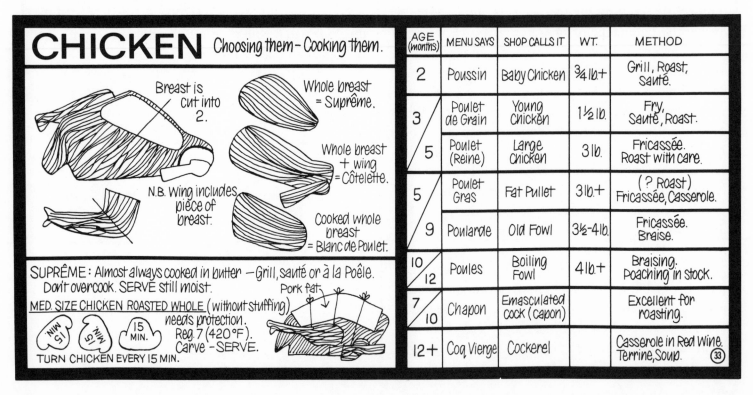

CHICKEN Choosing them – Cooking them.

Breast is cut into 2.

Whole breast = Suprême.

Whole breast + wing = Côtelette.

N.B. Wing includes piece of breast.

Cooked whole breast = Blanc de Poulet.

SUPRÊME: Almost always cooked in butter — Grill, sauté or à la Poêle. Don't overcook. SERVE still moist.

MED. SIZE CHICKEN ROASTED WHOLE (without stuffing) needs protection. Reg. 7 (420°F). Carve – SERVE.

Pork fat

15 MIN. / 15 MIN. / 15 MIN.

TURN CHICKEN EVERY 15 MIN.

AGE (months)	MENU SAYS	SHOP CALLS IT	WT.	METHOD
2	Poussin	Baby Chicken	¾ lb.+	Grill, Roast, Sauté.
3	Poulet de Grain	Young Chicken	1½ lb.	Fry, Sauté, Roast.
5	Poulet (Reine)	Large Chicken	3 lb.	Fricassée. Roast with care.
5	Poulet Gras	Fat Pullet	3 lb.+	(? Roast) Fricassée, Casserole.
9	Poularde	Old Fowl	3½–4 lb.	Fricassée. Braise.
10 / 12	Poules	Boiling Fowl	4 lb.+	Braising. Poaching in stock.
7 / 10	Chapon	Emasculated cock (capon)		Excellent for roasting.
12+	Coq Vierge	Cockerel		Casserole in Red Wine. Terrine, Soup.

A most excellent way of roasting a chicken is to butter the inside of the thin slice of pork fat that bards the breast. It adds great flavour but it's protected from heat and so can't burn. Chicken cooks very quickly. (Don't stuff it. If you want stuffing, cook it alongside the chicken). It's a good idea to cut the raw chicken into sections. That's not only easier than dissecting it on the table but gives you a chance to select certain parts for other recipes, e.g. a chicken without the *suprêmes* might be enough for a *sauté* or a *fricassée* and for the next meal the two *suprêmes* can do an impressive solo hammered flat, cooked gently for 7 or 8 minutes in clarified butter, then served with a good sauce or decorated in aspic.

The commonest error in preparing chicken is to overcook it. The flesh must be moist. Some cooks instruct that a needle inserted should run with yellow juice but not pink juices. That's O.K. in theory but in practice it's not a good idea to waste that juice, for it is the very essence of the chicken's flavour. Many chickens are deep-frozen. Cooks usually cook them immediately after thawing – in fact some cooks hardly give them a chance to thaw at all – but don't do that. Give the thawed chicken at least 24 hours hanging in a cool draughty place. That at least gives you a chance to compare it with a non-frozen one.

Tarragon is the classic accompaniment in France. Put a large sprig of it inside the bird while it's cooking. The cooking pan can be *déglacé* with any alcohol (e.g. dry white wine) and generous thick cream stirred into the resulting gravy. This is called *poulet à l'estragon*.

In Britain the nearest thing we have to the big *poularde* is a tough old fowl and so I've shown it. But in France a *poularde* is a specially fattened tender young hen, and so can be used in recipes that call for frying or grilling, etc.

Pot-roasting in the authentic French style

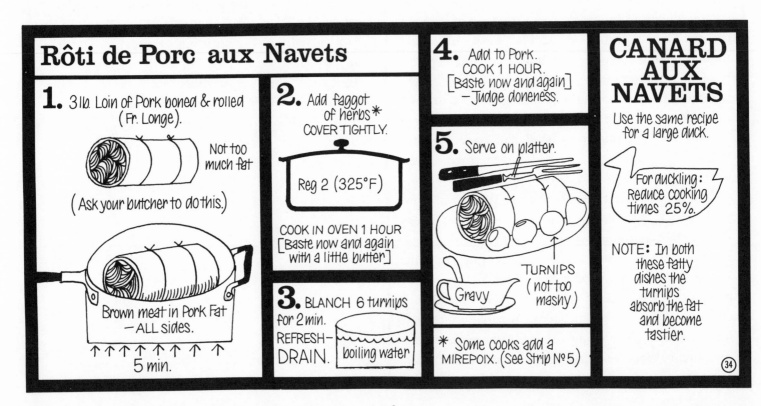

Rôti de Porc aux Navets

1. 3 lb. Loin of Pork boned & rolled (Fr. Longe).

Not too much fat

(Ask your butcher to do this.)

Brown meat in Pork Fat — ALL sides.

5 min.

2. Add faggot of herbs* COVER TIGHTLY.

Reg 2 (325°F)

COOK IN OVEN 1 HOUR [Baste now and again with a little butter]

3. BLANCH 6 turnips for 2 min. REFRESH— DRAIN. boiling water

4. Add to Pork. COOK 1 HOUR. [Baste now and again] —Judge doneness.

5. Serve on platter.

Gravy

TURNIPS (not too mashy)

* Some cooks add a MIREPOIX. (See Strip Nº 5)

CANARD AUX NAVETS

Use the same recipe for a large duck.

For duckling: Reduce cooking times 25%.

NOTE: In both these fatty dishes the turnips absorb the fat and become tastier.

③④

French butchers are very highly skilled, and although meat is expensive in France the preparation that it receives before it is sold goes some way to making up the difference in price. Because French kitchens favour the oval-shaped casserole pan many boned joints are trussed to this shape. Sometimes loin cuts that include the kidney are boned and rolled so that the kidney becomes the 'stuffing' inside the roll. This is called a *rognonnade*. In France the skin of pork is not served to the table on a roast joint. This is because the skin is a favourite ingredient and also because pigs in France are fattened well beyond English sizes and so a joint that kept the skin attached would have an enormous thickness of fat. So follow the French system: remove the skin and use it for flavouring a stew or soup. Remove thin slices of fat as evenly as you can and use them to bard a chicken or lean joint. For the loin of pork leave just $\frac{1}{8}$ inch layer of fat around it. Even then you may prefer to degrease the juice at the bottom of the casserole before adding the turnips.

There is a very similar recipe which has strips of Gruyère cheese and ham buried inside the rolled pork. When the pork is sliced the cheese will have melted into a sort of marble pattern. Any of these pork recipes are good – perhaps even better – cold. Pork is often served with sweet or fruity things, in Britain with apple sauce, in the U.S.A. with cranberry, pineapple or peaches; and even the French – in spite of all the things they say about such practices – serve gooseberry jelly with pork.

How to fry steaks, chops and any sliced meat

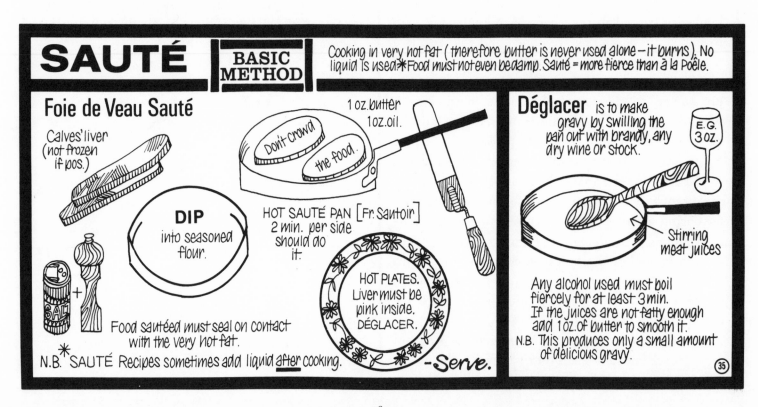

SAUTÉ **BASIC METHOD** Cooking in very hot fat (therefore butter is never used alone – it burns). No liquid is used.✱ Food must not even be damp. Sauté = more fierce than à la Poêle.

Foie de Veau Sauté

Calves' liver (not frozen if pos.)

1 oz. butter 1 oz. oil.

Don't crowd the food.

DIP into seasoned flour.

HOT SAUTÉ PAN [Fr. Sautoir] 2 min. per side should do it.

SALT +

Food sautéed must seal on contact with the very hot fat.

N.B. ✱ SAUTÉ Recipes sometimes add liquid after cooking.

HOT PLATES. Liver must be pink inside. DÉGLACER.

–Serve.

Déglacer is to make gravy by swilling the pan out with brandy, any dry wine or stock.

E.G. 3 OZ.

Stirring meat juices

Any alcohol used must boil fiercely for at least 3 min. If the juices are not fatty enough add 1 oz. of butter to smooth it. N.B. This produces only a small amount of delicious gravy.

㉟

You will be able to find plenty of recipes with the word *sauté* in the title that do not seem to be anything like this one. That is because the title is often taken from the method of preparation whatever process it goes through subsequently. This then is *sautéing*. It is especially good for liver where it's important to serve it underdone, but it can be applied to countless dishes from lamb chops or chicken breasts to cold boiled beef or chicken livers.

Page 112 tells the burning temperature of various sorts of cooking fat. Using an electric thermostat enables you to heat your chosen fat without worrying about burning it. The finest type of fat – most French cooks would say – is taken from around beef kidney. Pork fat taken from the loin near the skin or from the head is a close runner-up and preferred by some. Veal fat is not highly thought of except for certain rather specialized uses (no one has yet told me what those uses are!) and mutton fat is not worth saving.

Fish is usually cooked in oil, a notable exception being fish prepared *à la meunière*.

The object of any sort of frying (deep or *sauté*) is to have the fat so hot that it seals the food. This prevents fat entering the food, for this would make it soggy with fat, which is revolting. All frying consists of keeping the fat as hot as it can go without burning. Bear in mind that the raw food is cold and will cool the fat.

How a fricassée differs from a blanquette

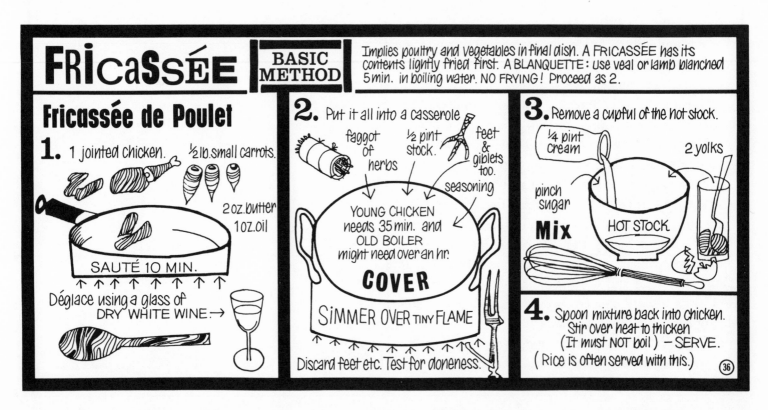

FRiCaSSÉE | **BASIC METHOD** — Implies poultry and vegetables in final dish. A FRICASSÉE has its contents lightly fried first. A BLANQUETTE: use veal or lamb blanched 5 min. in boiling water. NO FRYING! Proceed as 2.

Fricassée de Poulet

1. 1 jointed chicken. ½ lb. small carrots. 2 oz. butter 1 oz. oil

SAUTÉ 10 MIN.

Déglace using a glass of DRY WHITE WINE →

2. Put it all into a casserole — faggot of herbs, ½ pint stock, feet & giblets too, seasoning.

YOUNG CHICKEN needs 35 min. and OLD BOILER might need over an hr.

COVER

SIMMER OVER TINY FLAME

Discard feet etc. Test for doneness.

3. Remove a cupful of the hot stock. ¼ pint cream, 2 yolks, pinch sugar

Mix — HOT STOCK

4. Spoon mixture back into chicken. Stir over heat to thicken (It must NOT boil) – SERVE. (Rice is often served with this.)

(36)

I have known cooks with some pretty wild ideas about how *fricassées* differ from *blanquettes*, but the only difference is that for a *blanquette* the operation number one above is replaced by a blanching of the meat for 5 mins. in water. Discard the water, then proceed as in stage two. Confusion is fomented by some French chefs who seem to reserve the word *fricassée* for *fricassées* of chicken, but this is just a fashionable trend, so take no notice.

A *fricassée* or a *blanquette* can have a plain *béchamel* sauce substituted for the cream and egg yolks. In each case it will be acceptable and in each case equally incorrect.

If you substitute red wine for the stock and *déglace* with brandy you will have a *coq au vin*. No need to start off with a cockerel. But the long cooking time needed for a boiling fowl gives the wine a chance to mellow in flavour. In France it is usual to add a teaspoon of sugar to the wine for *coq au vin*.

A veal *fricassée* to a Frenchman is not worth the name unless it has a cut of veal called *tendron* in it. This is because this is the region of the crunchy false ribs. If you would like to use the same part, make sure that you are getting imported veal (English veal is generally far too young and tasteless) and get the middle (fore and aft wise) of the breast. If you don't want to try *tendron* use shoulder of veal. Poultry, rabbit, and lamb are also suitable for *fricassée* or *blanquette*. The French version of curry usually appears as a *fricassée*. *Fricassée de poulet à l'indienne*: a dessert-spoon of curry powder is cooked into the butter and oil at stage one. *Fricassée de poulet au paprika* is prepared exactly the same as *indienne*, except that one tablespoon best-quality paprika is used instead of curry powder.

Braised meat served hot or cold

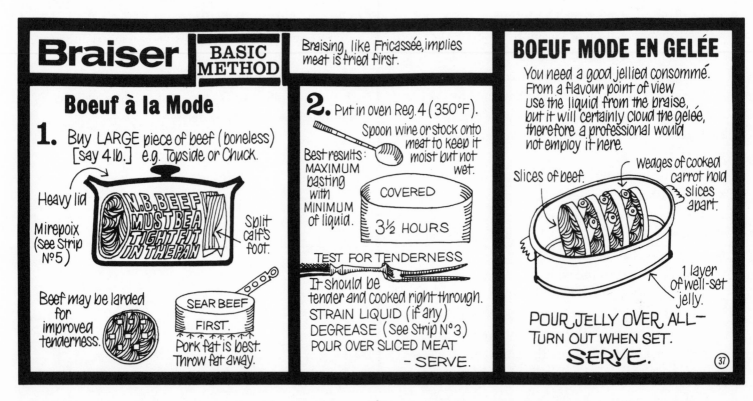

Braiser | **BASIC METHOD**

Braising, like Fricassée, implies meat is fried first.

Boeuf à la Mode

1. Buy LARGE piece of beef (boneless) [say 4 lb.] e.g. Topside or Chuck.

Heavy lid

Mirepoix (see Strip Nº 5)

N.B. BEEF MUST BE A TIGHT FIT IN THE PAN

Split calf's foot.

Beef may be larded for improved tenderness.

SEAR BEEF FIRST.

Pork fat is best. Throw fat away.

2. Put in oven Reg. 4 (350°F).

Spoon wine or stock onto meat to keep it moist but not wet.

Best results: MAXIMUM basting with MINIMUM of liquid.

COVERED

3½ HOURS

TEST FOR TENDERNESS

It should be tender and cooked right through. STRAIN LIQUID (if any) DEGREASE (See Strip Nº 3) POUR OVER SLICED MEAT – SERVE.

BOEUF MODE EN GELÉE

You need a good jellied consommé. From a flavour point of view use the liquid from the braise, but it will certainly cloud the gelée, therefore a professional would not employ it here.

slices of beef.

wedges of cooked carrot hold slices apart.

1 layer of well-set jelly.

POUR JELLY OVER ALL— TURN OUT WHEN SET.

SERVE.

③⑦

Braiser is often translated as stewing but the two processes have very little in common. *Braisage* is much more like English pot-roasting. Remember it should have a maximum of basting with a minimum of liquid. Ideally the meat should be kept moist by adding a spoonful of good stock from time to time. The basting must not wash the meat juices away. The final result should be a moist piece of meat, shiny and glazed with a crust of the stock plus the juices from inside the meat that cooking (i.e. shrinkage) has forced to the surface. It is sliced like a very tender roast joint. The gravy should be minimal.

In olden times braising was done in a *braisière*, which was a strange metal pot on legs. It stood in the fire. Around the lid of the pot were ridges so that red-hot coals could be propped on top of it. It could remain there all night using the dying warmth of the fire. Nowadays the temperature can be carefully adjusted to give you a result as quick as you want it; but slow cooking will pay off.

To enjoy braised meat at its most delicious put a leg of beef, cut into one-inch cubes, into a tightly closed pot. Cook in an oven at 200°F. for 4 or 5 hours. It needs no moisture but a chopped onion included with raw meat cubes increases the gravy.

Cuire à l'étuvée is a process rather like braising except that no liquid is added to the food in the pot and only butter is used as a cooking medium. Because *étuvée* means that the temperature must remain below the boiling point of water (212°F.) it is usually a process for cooking vegetables like lettuce, peas, or celery, or meat or poultry that has been cut into pieces. *A la poêle* is the same as *à l'étuvée*.

Marinaded meat cooked in a closed pot

A DAUBE Same as ESTOUFFADE. Almost always marinaded first. NEVER FRIED. Can be whole piece or cut up as here. Former is always larded first.

BASIC METHOD

LARDING:

Fresh pork fat.

↕ 1/4"

Larding needle.

cube larded.

Thin bards of pork fat outside makes it even better.

↕ 2"

← 2" →

Soak LARDONS overnight in brandy before use.

Cut lardons (strips) flush if you like.

MARINADE:

Steep meat overnight.

1 carrot

2 tablespoons olive oil

1/2 bottle any dry wine

Bouquet Garni

1 chopped onion

bay

2 oz. brandy

clove garlic

Turn meat sometimes.

a daube: Use beef

or pork. Eat hot or cold.

Add 1 pint marinade or stock, faggot herbs + lot of garlic.

Thin slices 1/2 lb. pork belly, 3 lb. beef (or pork) in cubes, 1/2 lb. sliced mushroom, 1 1/2 lb. chopped tomato.

Flour + water to make a seal

STICK LID ON

3 hrs at Reg 3 (325°F).

38

Every region of France boasts a dish of this sort and each has its variations; pork, mutton, beef, and duck can be cooked this way. Sometimes the meat is in one piece and sometimes cut up, but it is always marinaded before cooking and usually cooked in the marinade liquid. If it's in a large piece the meat must be larded first. If it's cut up, larding is optional. By tradition a *daubière* was a heavy pot with a well-fitting lid. Any such pot will do, but for the best results the meat must fit fairly closely into it. It can be cooked at any temperature but lower temperature and longer cooking gives the best result. (Try cooking a three-pound cut of beef for five hours at the lowest setting on your oven). With those rules in mind you can invent your own combinations.

When you are using a marinade remember that a cooked marinade (*marinade cuite*) works more quickly than an ordinary one. You can use the same ingredients but lightly fry the vegetables and after adding the rest of the ingredients simmer it about thirty minutes. Use it when it's cold.

If you haven't used a larding needle before, push the needle through once without fat (to make a hole), then push it through with fat on. Watch carefully or you'll forget where it went. Don't be in a hurry until you get the knack of it and try to get fat evenly through the meat, i.e. don't bother to put a *lardon* where natural fat occurs already. A professional cook doesn't cut the ends flush; in fact, he deliberately leaves long ends of fat outside the meat.

Estouffades and *daubes* are just as good cold as they are hot, and in ancient times the *daube* was always a cold dish. A cold *daube* of pork is superb but, like all *daubes*, it might need degreasing.

All you need to know about steak

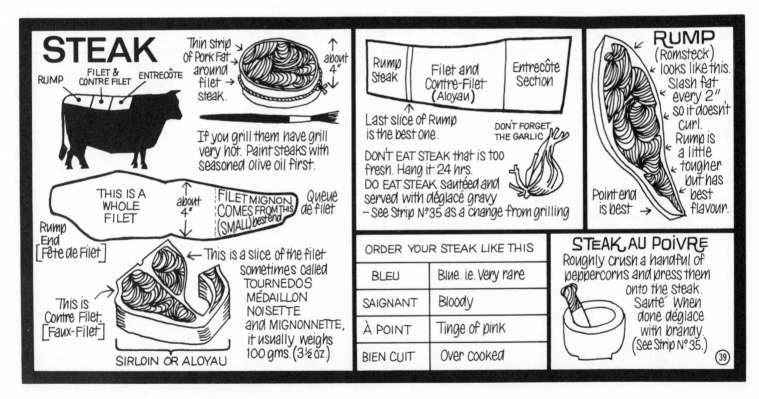

STEAK

RUMP — FILET & CONTRE FILET — ENTRECÔTE

Thin strip of Pork Fat around filet steak. about 4"

If you grill them have grill very hot. Paint steaks with seasoned olive oil first.

THIS IS A WHOLE FILET — about 4"

Rump End [Fête de Filet]

FILET MIGNON COMES FROM THIS (SMALL) best end — Queue de filet

This is Contre Filet. [Faux-Filet]

← This is a slice of the filet sometimes called TOURNEDOS MÉDAILLON NOISETTE and MIGNONNETTE, it usually weighs 100 gms. (3½ oz.)

SIRLOIN OR ALOYAU

| Rump Steak | Filet and Contre-Filet (Aloyau) | Entrecôte Section |

Last slice of Rump is the best one.

DON'T EAT STEAK that is too fresh. Hang it 24 hrs.
DO EAT STEAK sautéed and served with déglacé gravy
— See Strip N°35 as a change from grilling

DON'T FORGET THE GARLIC

RUMP (Romsteck) looks like this. Slash fat every 2" so it doesn't curl. Rump is a little tougher but has best flavour.

Point end is best

ORDER YOUR STEAK LIKE THIS	
BLEU	Blue. ie. Very rare
SAIGNANT	Bloody
À POINT	Tinge of pink
BIEN CUIT	Over cooked

STEAK AU POIVRE
Roughly crush a handful of peppercorns and press them onto the steak. Sauté. When done déglace with brandy. (See Strip N°35.)

(39)

This is just the basic information about steaks. The fillet is the most famous and most expensive; some cooks roast a whole *filet* and serve it like a joint, but it needs lots of larding and I don't think it makes a successful roast. What's more, it worries the cook sick while it's cooking. A sirloin on the bone is a better roast, either with or without the *filet* section still attached to it. Have your butcher cut slices from the sirloin which can be served with or without the piece of *filet*. (N.B. A sirloin is not exactly the same as *aloyau*.)

Contre-filet is sometimes served in France under the name *Romsteck* or *Entrecôte*, but the latter name is more strictly only to be used for a slice of meat taken from between the bones of wing rib of beef. An *entrecôte minute* is a very thin steak cooked quickly, but not necessarily thin enough to cook in only one minute. For something a little more elaborate than *déglacé* gravy put a *sauce béarnaise* (page 136) on your steak or make a *sauce madère* (page 130) and add lots of mushrooms to it. This is called *bifteck sauté chasseur*. There are hundreds of more complex garnishes for steak, but I don't recommend any of them unless the steak is so poor it needs dressing up.

Lastly, make sure that your steak is well hung before it's cooked; most steaks need 24 hours' hanging after purchase. Season a good steak only with freshly-ground pepper and sea salt (*gros sel*). The latter should not be put on until after cooking, since it draws the moisture out, and cooking any steak is a process of retaining the maximum amount of juice inside it.

The French way with hamburger

Bifteck Haché

1. 2½ lb. of entirely lean chuck ground by butcher N.B. No gristle, tendons, etc.

egg

seasoning

salt

¼ lb. of any of these. { Best beef suet. Marrow from marrow bone Butter (least suitable).

2. FORM INTO STEAKS

1"

2"

SAUTÉ (see Strip Nº 35)

SERVE with déglacé gravy or go to town with a fancy sauce — e.g. Madère (Strip Nº 10) Béarnaise Colbert Choron } Strip Nº 13

à la tartare (Steak served uncooked)

Buy 6 oz. good quality lean steak per person. Have it ground by butcher, then season it with salt and pepper.

Raw egg yolk in hollow.

Strips of anchovy.

Garnish with:

tomato cucumber

raw onion capers

SERVE WITH WORCESTERSHIRE sauce.

40

190

The meat ball is just as frequently found in France as it is elsewhere. This is because finely chopped or ground meat is economical and versatile. A skilled shopper chooses the meat, then asks the butcher to grind it, rather than buys ready-ground meat from the tray, because that is likely to be second-rate meat. Ground meat does not keep well and should be used on the day of purchase. If it is put into a refrigerator it should be forked over and spread out, because the particles of air trapped inside the piled-up meat will go stale and turn the meat bad very quickly.

Small meat balls can be grilled, sautéed, dipped in batter and deep-fried, poached in *bouillon* (use the *bouillon* afterwards, for a lot of the flavour will be lost into it), or wrapped in very thin dough (that prevents the flavour escaping) and poached in *bouillon* or steamed. They can be served with any of the sauces mentioned below or sour cream or a purée of tomato sometimes called a *coulis*. Such a purée is made by putting half a pound of roughly chopped tomatoes, a big knob of butter, seasoning and a tablespoonful of chopped onion in a closed saucepan over a tiny flame. After about an hour, strain the purée (a Mouli is useful here) and adjust seasoning. You may need a pinch of sugar. This tomato *coulis* is a useful all-round sauce for fish, meat or poultry. It's very little trouble to prepare – apart from the final straining – because there is no need to skin the tomatoes.

N.B. Don't quote me, but tomatoes slightly less than fresh can be used up in this way. If you add vinegar, sugar, pepper, and spices and let it cool down you'll have tomato ketchup.

Preparing meat for the pot

STUFFED MEAT

Get your butcher to bone it — then proceed.

French Cooks usually prefer to braise these joints. If you have a large pot do the same.

A shoulder or Leg of Veal can be given the same treatment.

LEG OF LAMB

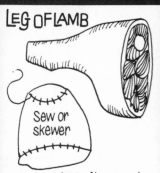

Sew or skewer

Use a highly flavoured stuffing. (e.g. lamb – kidney, breadcrumbs, egg and Rosemary); it will need about 20 min. per lb. + 20 min. roasting — SERVE hot.

BREAST OF VEAL

Don't open here.

open this end – then sew it up.

Use any good stuffing.
[Pork e.g. See Strip N°31]
Roast it over 3 hrs at Reg. 3 (330°F) — Serve hot OR cold.

SHOULDER OF LAMB

Tie it like this

The leg stuffing would suit this too. It will need about 2¾ hrs roasting at Reg 3 (330°F) — SERVE hot.

PAUPIETTE OF VEAL

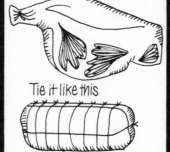

CHEESE
HAM
VEAL SLICE (from fillet end of leg?)
Thump it well.
Toothpick

Braise gently, moistening with dry white wine. 1 hr at Reg 3 (330°F) SERVE hot.

OISEAUX SANS TÊTE

stuffing

Very thin slice of Rump Steak.

Stuff with chopped bacon and ham. Cook with tomatoes and mushrooms as Daube recipe Strip 38. SERVE hot.

(41)

No French cook will put anything into an oven if he can get it in a pot. This probably stems from the tradition of country cooking in which kitchens often have no oven, only an open fire. Even today in country districts oven-cooked dishes are considered too sophisticated for everyday eating; for, unlike British country cooking, it is very unusual for a French household to bake its own bread. So if you want to be authentic you will cook these joints of meat in a large iron pot. The oval-shaped pot is popular in France, for it takes poultry, and the other joints (like stuffed shoulder, below) are tied to fit into it whenever they can be. Ideally the meat should fit quite closely to the pot with perhaps an inch or so space. There should be a bed of fried onion or a *mirepoix* (page 120) under the meat.

There are countless variations of stuffing (see page 172) ranging from merely using ground meat of the same type as the joint to all kinds of herbs and flavourings including anchovy, chopped olives, chestnut purée, ginger, kidney, or liver. The stuffed meat will be a little easier to carve if you rest it for fifteen minutes in a warm place before carving it. This gives the meat a chance to settle down and the stuffing becomes a little more firm. Stuffed joints of this sort are also good for a cold buffet. In that case don't cut them until they are quite cold or a lot of the flavour and juice will escape.

The cuts of meat in France don't provide a shoulder that is suitable for stuffing, so stuffed lamb in France is usually a leg. A loin is often stuffed so that the kidney remains as a stuffing inside it. If you do this be sure that the fat around the kidney is trimmed to a minimum.

Cooking vegetables the French way

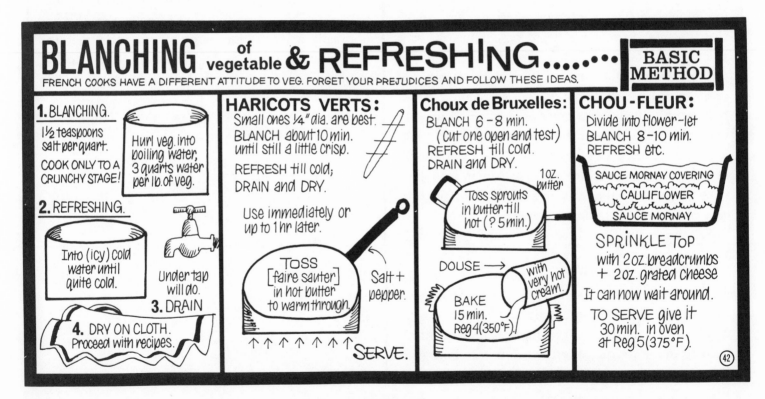

BLANCHING of vegetable **& REFRESHING........** | BASIC METHOD

FRENCH COOKS HAVE A DIFFERENT ATTITUDE TO VEG. FORGET YOUR PREJUDICES AND FOLLOW THESE IDEAS.

1. BLANCHING.
1½ teaspoons salt per quart.
COOK ONLY TO A CRUNCHY STAGE!

Hurl veg. into boiling water, 3 quarts water per lb. of veg.

2. REFRESHING.
Into (icy) cold water until quite cold.

Under tap will do.

3. DRAIN

4. DRY ON CLOTH. Proceed with recipes.

HARICOTS VERTS:
Small ones ¼" dia. are best.
BLANCH about 10 min. until still a little crisp.

REFRESH till cold; DRAIN and DRY.

Use immediately or up to 1 hr later.

TOSS [faire sauter] in hot butter to warm through.

Salt + pepper.

↑ ↑ ↑ ↑ ↑ ↑ ↑ SERVE.

Choux de Bruxelles:
BLANCH 6 – 8 min.
(Cut one open and test)
REFRESH till cold.
DRAIN and DRY.

1 oz. butter

Toss sprouts in butter till hot (? 5 min.)

DOUSE →

with very hot cream.

BAKE 15 min. Reg 4 (350°F).

CHOU - FLEUR:
Divide into flower-let
BLANCH 8–10 min.
REFRESH etc.

SAUCE MORNAY COVERING
CAULIFLOWER
SAUCE MORNAY

SPRINKLE TOP with 2 oz. breadcrumbs + 2 oz. grated cheese

It can now wait around.

TO SERVE give it 30 min. in oven at Reg 5 (375°F).

(42)

Although it may not be what many people think of as French cooking, this process of blanching and refreshing is the standard method of handling vegetables in France. Quite apart from any other consideration it's a great advantage to be able to leave the drained and dried vegetables for up to an hour before warming them briskly in butter.

N.B. Don't press the juice from the vegetable when drying it. Naturally enough there isn't a method of preparation that will make poor, soft, discoloured, old vegetables taste good, so choose carefully when you buy. Brussels sprouts, peas, *courgettes*, and beans are best when small and compact. Cabbage should be heavy. Vegetables washed with high-power sprays are seldom as flavourful as dirty ones, although they are very convenient.

The vegetables shown aren't the only ones suitable for this method. Do the same with carrots, celery, celeriac, asparagus, French beans, garden peas, broccoli, and many other things. Small variations in flavouring will ring the changes on vegetables when the choice is poor. Basil is great on peas or string beans and almost a must on a tomato. Bay goes with just about everything but is especially good with onion or carrots. Chervil can be used almost as widely as parsley is now. Mint is also too restricted in use; try it on string beans, spinach, or carrots as a change from on potato and peas. For another change, warm the vegetable in cream or sour cream in place of butter. Frozen vegetables have all been blanched and refreshed before being frozen. For this reason they can often be merely lightly warmed in butter after they are thawed.

Vegetables cooked slowly for extra flavour

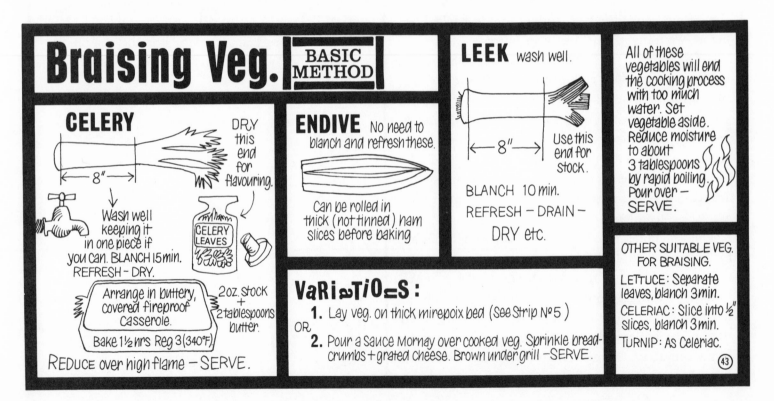

Braising Veg. BASIC METHOD

CELERY

DRY this end for flavouring.

8"

Wash well keeping it in one piece if you can. BLANCH 15min. REFRESH – DRY.

CELERY LEAVES

Arrange in buttery, covered fireproof casserole.

2oz. stock + 2 tablespoons butter.

Bake 1½ hrs Reg 3(340°F).

REDUCE over high flame – SERVE.

ENDIVE No need to blanch and refresh these.

Can be rolled in thick (not tinned) ham slices before baking

VaRiⱥTiOꞓS:

1. Lay veg. on thick mirepoix bed (see Strip Nº 5)

OR

2. Pour a sauce Mornay over cooked veg. Sprinkle breadcrumbs + grated cheese. Brown under grill – SERVE.

LEEK wash well.

8"

Use this end for stock.

BLANCH 10 min.

REFRESH – DRAIN –

DRY etc.

All of these vegetables will end the cooking process with too much water. Set vegetable aside. Reduce moisture to about 3 tablespoons by rapid boiling. Pour over – SERVE.

OTHER SUITABLE VEG. FOR BRAISING.

LETTUCE: Separate leaves, blanch 3min.

CELERIAC: Slice into ½" slices, blanch 3min.

TURNIP: As Celeriac.

(43)

Anything can be braised if you wait long enough. Cooking at these low temperatures the food will retain its maximum amount of moisture and in fact will often end up with a little too much moisture, as mentioned in the strip. If you want to take this a stage further you can make sure that the oven heat is below the boiling point of water (212° F.) so that none of the water will change into steam. This is called cooking *étuvée* (menus say *à la poêle*) and there is an unbreakable rule that no liquid must be added, although you can splash lots of melted butter around. Whole lettuce or garden peas, or sometimes those two mixed together, are often cooked this way and even they will take a long time, perhaps an hour and a half. Meat cooked this way takes so long that it's almost always cut up.

Braising however is not as slow as that. Endive will be ready in about an hour. Lemon-juice, butter, sugar, and salt will improve it. Endive (sometimes called chicory in Britain) changes flavour as it cooks. Sauerkraut also becomes milder and more mellow with braising, especially if you use a really good stock or white wine. Celery is another vegetable which will change in texture and flavour while it's cooking; that's why recipes vary so much in the cooking times they give. Celery is, of course, good to eat raw and also good when it's cooked almost to a pulp. Decide how you like it by experiment but remember that the cardinal rule of all braising is maximum basting with minimum liquid.

Vegetables with very little meat

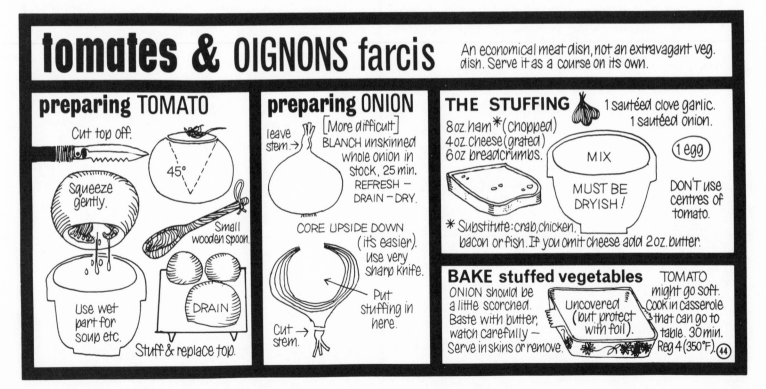

tomates & OIGNONS farcis

An economical meat dish, not an extravagant veg. dish. Serve it as a course on its own.

preparing TOMATO

Cut top off.

45°

Squeeze gently.

Small wooden spoon.

Use wet part for soup etc.

DRAIN

Stuff & replace top.

preparing ONION

leave stem →

[More difficult]
BLANCH unskinned whole onion in stock, 25 min.
REFRESH – DRAIN – DRY.

CORE UPSIDE DOWN
(it's easier).
Use very sharp knife.

Put stuffing in here.

Cut → stem.

THE STUFFING

1 sautéed clove garlic.
1 sautéed onion.

8 oz. ham * (chopped)
4 oz. cheese (grated)
6 oz. breadcrumbs.

MIX

MUST BE DRYISH!

1 egg

DON'T use centres of tomato.

* Substitute: crab, chicken, bacon or fish. If you omit cheese add 2 oz. butter.

BAKE stuffed vegetables

ONION should be a little scorched. Baste with butter, watch carefully — Serve in skins or remove.

Uncovered (but protect with foil).

TOMATO might go soft. Cook in casserole that can go to table. 30 min. Reg 4 (350°F). (44)

This is another one of those dishes designed to eke out small purchases of expensive meat. Don't therefore serve it as a special vegetable alongside a piece of steak; serve it as a solo. Probably about the simplest filling for stuffed vegetables of this sort is a raw egg. Bake the vegetable gently until the egg-white goes opaque. The most common mistake is to include the moist content of the tomatoes, which will make them sag; so will topping the tomatoes too low down. Some cooks add a little stock (or even water) to the dish in which the baking takes place so that the resulting steam will help it cook.

Cooked rice is a popular item to add to the stuffings. Some recipes use one teaspoonful of raw rice and two teaspoonsful of stock so that the rice actually cooks inside the vegetable. You'll need a moderate oven and it will take about an hour.

Tomatoes *Provençal* style is about the most economical of all. They are stuffed with breadcrumbs, parsley, lots of crushed garlic and lots of olive oil. If you want to serve the vegetables cold (this especially applies to tomatoes), there are all sorts of combinations using mayonnaise and cold cooked vegetables or chopped hard-boiled egg. *Aspics* can also be made from stuffed, baked vegetables, for instance chopped, cooked, jellied pork can be put inside a tomato while it's hot. The tomato can itself be glazed with a jelly or put into a cup, jelly poured all over it, and unmoulded when set. Using a jellied stuffing for vegetables that will be served cold makes them rather solid and so especially suitable for a picnic dish.

A short course in picking and eating mushrooms

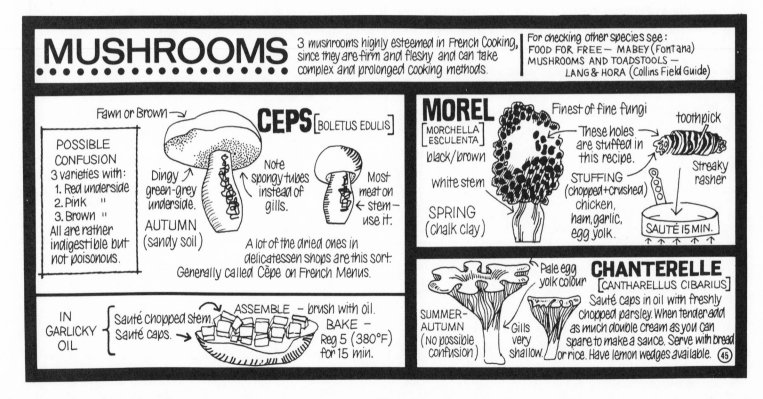

MUSHROOMS 3 mushrooms highly esteemed in French Cooking, since they are firm and fleshy and can take complex and prolonged cooking methods.

For checking other species see:
FOOD FOR FREE — MABEY (Fontana)
MUSHROOMS AND TOADSTOOLS —
LANG & HORA (Collins Field Guide)

CEPS [BOLETUS EDULIS]

Fawn or Brown

POSSIBLE CONFUSION
3 varieties with:
1. Red underside
2. Pink "
3. Brown "
All are rather indigestible but not poisonous.

Dingy green-grey underside.

AUTUMN (sandy soil)

Note spongy tubes instead of gills.

Most meat on stem — use it.

A lot of the dried ones in delicatessen shops are this sort. Generally called Cêpe on French Menus.

IN GARLICKY OIL { Sauté chopped stem. Sauté caps.

ASSEMBLE — brush with oil.
BAKE — Reg 5 (380°F) for 15 min.

MOREL
[MORCHELLA ESCULENTA]
black/brown
white stem
SPRING (chalk clay)

Finest of fine fungi

These holes are stuffed in this recipe.

toothpick

Streaky rasher

STUFFING (chopped+crushed) chicken, ham, garlic, egg yolk.

SAUTÉ 15 MIN.

CHANTERELLE [CANTHARELLUS CIBARIUS]

Pale egg yolk colour

SUMMER-AUTUMN (no possible confusion)

Gills very shallow.

Sauté caps in oil with freshly chopped parsley. When tender add as much double cream as you can spare to make a sauce. Serve with bread or rice. Have lemon wedges available. (45)

There are plenty of theories about how to tell an edible fungus from a non-edible one but these theories are seldom expounded by collectors. For good reason. There is no golden rule. None of those stories about turning the silver black, being easy to peel or easy to take the stalk off are worth a damn. The only way is to know by identification. Luckily for the gourmet the types that have developed a reputation through the ages – for the Romans were great fungi eaters – are quite distinctive in appearance.

The three I have shown are easy to recognize, and I have shown which are likely to be found where and when. If you buy yourself a book on the subject – I especially recommend one that has coloured pictures to give you confidence – then you will be able to recognize many others that are equally edible. Most of the ones listed as inedible are merely unpleasant to eat, or at least might give you indigestion (but it's true that there are poisonous mushrooms).

When your mushrooms are collected and identified examine them carefully for mushroom worms. I dare say you have come across even cultivated mushrooms with their tiny latticework of channels, so you'll know what to look for. Rinse the mushrooms briefly in acidulated water (that's a pint of water with a couple of tablespoons of vinegar in it) and pay particular attention to the morels, which seem to get grimier than the others.

From now on you are on your own. Sauté them in butter, put them in pies or *vol-au-vent* cases, wrap them in ham, serve them in cream, in omelette, in salad. They don't keep very long, so go on, have some more.

Endless variations on the potato

POTATO

GALETTE de Pommes de Terre

1. 2lb. potatoes – DRY VERY THIN SLICES.

Make them with a peeler?

Lay them in a buttered pan.

1 oz. butter
1 oz. oil
seasoning.

Make it very hot, then turn to very tiny flame. COOK 20 min.

2. Turn it over to cook other side.

A plate makes it easier.

Cook till crusty outside, cooked inside (?10 min.) SERVE.

Pommes de Terre DUCHESSE

BOIL 1lb. potatoes, DRAIN them, SKIN – then ADD:

2oz. melted butter,
dust of nutmeg,
3 beaten egg yolks,
salt & pepper.

FORCING BAG

MASH WELL

SERVE or PIPE to decorate.

POTATO CROQUETTES

Form it into shapes.

1" ← 2½" →

Roll in egg + crumbs. Sauté – SERVE.

CROQUETTES POMMES DE TERRE À LA LYONNAISE.
Add chopped sautéed onion + chopped parsley.

à la PARMESANE Add grated Parmesan.

The French are just as crazy about potatoes as the English or the Irish. The French cook goes for the *duchesse* recipe because it is the potato in its most adaptable form. In a restaurant kitchen the piping bag is used more for *duchesse* potatoes than it is for piping frostings or cream. Shapes twirled across the top of a dish just before it is popped beneath the grill means that the fluted edges of potato will come out crispy brown and especially appetizing. A professional knocks out roses, ovals, surrounds, tiny loaves, and all shapes of croquette. The simplest of stews served inside a ring of piped plain *duchesse* can look very elegant. Piped potatoes won't make up for a dish that has gone wrong, and decoration of any kind must never be fussy or laboured; but then you knew that already.

Pommes de terre Anna is the same recipe as the *gallette* recipe here but it is cooked in the oven instead of on the stove-top. It is cooked tightly covered for about an hour (depending upon how deeply you pile the potato slices). If you want to avoid turning it over just tip it out upside-down and serve it like that. Both recipes sometimes have layers of flavourings between the potato slices. A *mirepoix*, grated cheese, spinach, mushrooms, or ham are all good. *Gallettes* can be any size at all. Small ones are used for garnish or as a base for an *escalope* or fillet steak.

Pommes de terre duchesse is sometimes shaped into little boats, brushed with beaten egg, and cooked till brown in a hot oven; when used as a garnish these are also called *gallettes de pomme de terre*. I'm sorry if that adds to your confusion, but there it is.

Custard the French way, and super custards

SWEET sauces Crème à l'Anglaise = A sauce. Butter Cream = A filling. Crème Collée = A glaze.

Crème à l'Anglaise

1. Scald (almost boil)

8 oz. milk * + 8 oz. cream.

BEAT FIRST!

2 teaspoons cornflour + 4 eggs + 2 oz. sugar.

BEAT

When sugar is dissolved —

STRAIN.

* A vanilla pod in the milk is great.

2. COOK OVER WATER

↑ ↑ ↑ ↑ ↑

— IT MUST NOT BOIL. When thick and creamy it's ready.

BUTTER CREAM is soft ½ lb. unsalted butter beaten a spoonful at a time into the COLD or tepid Crème à l'Anglaise.

CRÈME COLLÉE Dissolve 1 tablespoon of gelatine in a little water. Stir this into a Crème à l'Anglaise AFTER Stage 2.

CRÈME BAVAROISE Make Crème à l'Anglaise using 8 egg yolks. Then after Stage 2 add gelatine (as for Collée.) When result is cool (not cold) fold in 4 well-beaten egg whites, and ½ pint thickly whipped cream. REFRIGERATE IN MOULD.

TURN OUT SERVE

FLAVOURED VERSIONS have chosen flavouring added to milk of Crème à l'Anglaise E.G. 2 oz. melted chocolate, 1 tablespoon of instant coffee or brandy or liqueur.

(47)

Here are the whole group of French cream sauces. As you can see they are all based on *crème à l'anglaise*, which is a type of egg custard and should be used if you want to pour something over the prunes. There is no trick to making the *crème à l'anglaise* except keep the thing hot but never let it boil. Almost always when people have trouble with it this is because they haven't put the two teaspoons of corn-flour in. They feel it's cheating, that egg custard must never have flour of any kind near it. The sentiment is a noble one but it makes the job more difficult, for without that cornflour the mixture is far less stable and will react to heat variations of the slightest degree.

Choose the mixture according to what you need: if you are filling some *choux* pastry balls use butter cream, for something that will hold firm you'll need the *crème bavaroise*. The butter cream is one of many slightly different types; this one could pedantically be described as '*crème au beurre à l'anglaise*' and is interchangeable in use with any other that I have ever seen.

Any sort of flavouring can be used that won't affect the milk or eggs; some of the French com-mercial syrups are useful. If you use a vanilla pod, leave it immersed in the hot milk; it should be left standing about an hour. The used vanilla pod should be rinsed in warm water, dried carefully and can be used several times until the flavour is gone.

Making super custards into sublime desserts

BAVAROISE & CHARLOTTE RUSSE

You see why Crème Bavaroise needs yolks and gelatine if it's not to sag or collapse.

Bavaroise is just a Crème Bavaroise in a mould.

VARIATIONS: Sometimes have crushed purées of fruit stirred into them.

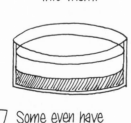

Some even have various layers.

Charlotte Russe

1. Buttered dish—

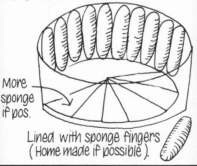

More sponge if pos.

Lined with sponge fingers (Home made if possible).

2. Pour vanilla flavoured Crème Bavaroise into a mould. Chill very well—turn out—SERVE.

Charlotte Nesselrode

As Charlotte Russe but a quarter of its bulk is chopped marrons glacés stirred into the CRÈME BAVAROISE

Charlotte Montreuil

As Nesselrode but chopped peaches instead of the marrons glacés.

INVENT YOUR OWN CHARLOTTE KIT!

Some recipes have the sponge fingers dipped in a flavouring (e.g. Coffee). If you do this add gelatine to the flavouring or you'll be in trouble!!!

(48)

If you put *Crème bavaroise* into a mould, chill it and then unmould it, the result is called a *bavaroise*. If that's too simple for you, then you can invent all sorts of variations. A typical variant is Bavarian cream *à la Normande*, which is a Calvados-flavoured *crème* with a filling of thick apple sauce that has been whisked carefully with gelatine (that has been dissolved in water) and a little thick cream stirred in finally. A favourite of mine is to put chopped ginger as a jellied base.

Whenever people ask for the recipe of *bavaroise* or *charlotte russe* I find they always say 'Well, of course it tastes good if it contains all that cream,' as though using luxury ingredients was cheating. If it's cheating, cheat.

I prefer *charlotte russe* to a *bavaroise*, especially if the sponge fingers are home-made and are dipped into a well-flavoured jelly. Try vanilla cream with coffee-flavoured fingers, or chocolate cream with coffee fingers. If that's a little too rich, use a sharp-flavoured lemon jelly for the fingers. Some cooks dribble the coffee jelly over the sponge fingers in arabesques so that the finished dish has a marbled appearance.

Home-made ice-cream 'cakes'

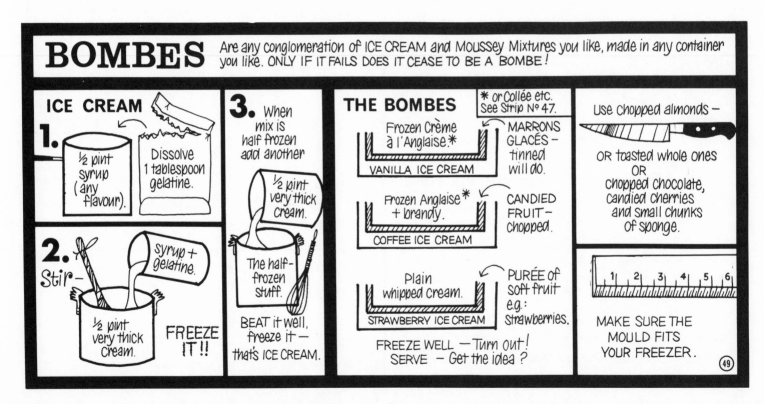

BOMBES Are any conglomeration of ICE CREAM and MOUSSEY Mixtures you like, made in any container you like. ONLY IF IT FAILS DOES IT CEASE TO BE A BOMBE!

ICE CREAM

1. ½ pint syrup (any flavour).

Dissolve 1 tablespoon gelatine.

2. Stir— syrup + gelatine. ½ pint very thick cream.

3. When mix is half frozen add another ½ pint very thick cream. The half-frozen stuff.

BEAT it well, freeze it — that's ICE CREAM.

FREEZE IT!!

THE BOMBES

* or Collée etc. See Strip N° 47.

Frozen Crème à l'Anglaise.* — MARRONS GLACÉS - tinned will do.
VANILLA ICE CREAM

Frozen Anglaise* + brandy. — CANDIED FRUIT - chopped.
COFFEE ICE CREAM

Plain whipped cream. — PURÉE of soft fruit e.g.: strawberries.
STRAWBERRY ICE CREAM

FREEZE WELL — Turn out!
SERVE — Get the idea?

Use chopped almonds —
OR toasted whole ones
OR chopped chocolate, candied cherries and small chunks of sponge.

1 2 3 4 5 6

MAKE SURE THE MOULD FITS YOUR FREEZER.

(49)

The traditional spherical shape of ice-cream *bombes* dates from the time when men in long beards with 'ski' at the end of their names hid these gadgets, still smoking, beneath ankle-length cloaks. Nowadays when bombs come in such a wide variety of shapes and sizes their culinary counterparts can do the same. Cake tins, bread tins, bowls, or basins are all suitable. In the commercial production of ice-cream the mixture is turned gently while freezing in order to prevent tiny daggers of ice forming inside it. There are tiny versions of these electric-motor-driven devices now available for domestic use, but any guest who doesn't prefer home-made ice-cream – daggers or no daggers – to commercial stuff shouldn't be served any.

You'll need a cold place to make ice-cream. If you have a freezer or a large refrigerator with a big freezing section there are no problems, but with a tiny refrigerator you will probably be better off to put the *bombe* into a polythene bag and bury it in a sack of ice. A three-quarter-pint size *bombe* will need at least four hours. There is probably a local ice company who will supply a sack of ice to your order. If you have trouble locating an ice company ask your fishmonger where he gets his ice.

You don't have to stop at the simple three-layer jobs I have shown here. Build six or seven layers of various colours, textures, and fruits. On the other hand two different flavourings will entitle you to use the word *bombe*. Remember that alcohol makes things more difficult to freeze, which is why anti-freeze goes into motor-car radiators in winter. So either take it easy on the booze or step up the cold.

Making fruit salad. A quick, inexpensive luxury dessert from 6 eggs

SYRUP

Poach fruit (fresh or dried) in syrup (Dried fruit must be soaked first) It is then called A COMPOTE.

SIMPLE SYRUP

1. STIR

2½ lb. sugar.

1 pint boiling water.

WAIT 24 hrs till sugar dissolves.

In FRANCE (and some specialised shops here) you can buy bottled syrups of all flavours. They are very useful. Get some if possible.

2. If you want a flavoured syrup

1. COFFEE: Add 2 heaped tablespoons of Instant Coffee.

2. VANILLA: Leave a vanilla pod in the syrup for 2–3 weeks

3. FRUIT: Use strained fruit juice instead of water. Fruit syrup made this way won't keep.

2–3 tablespoons alcohol can also be added.

SABAYON

A little older, it is thought, than its Italian counterpart – ZABAGLIONE.

6 raw yolks

6 teaspoons sugar

When it's nice and thick –

ADD 6 half shells of Madeira OR any sweet white wine.

HOT WATER

↑ Tiny flame ↑

BEAT till thick and fluffy.

SERVE HOT OR COLD – in which case beat a few times while it's cooling.

(50)

As with most of the recipes in this book I have given one simple method of making a *compote* and left the variations up to you. Vanilla, lemon-zest, orange-zest, cinnamon, and clove are some of the obvious things to use. If it's to be consumed immediately (within 24 hours) you can use any sort of juice as a flavouring. The syrups sold in France (and in some shops here) are so good that many cooks would not think of making a syrup unless it was the very simplest type. Dried fruit makes very successful *compotes*, apricot being a favourite one.

Sabayon is one of the most useful dessert dishes I know. When you have no fruit, no cream, and no liqueur or brandy, *sabayon* can save your reputation even if it's based on only a little sweet white wine. There is a great deal of nonsense talked about the alcohol content of this dish. There is no earthly reason for using a first-class sherry or worrying where to get Marsala when the taste is going to be drenched in sugar. Any white wine will do as long as it has no defect. There is no need to have an electric beater, a hand beater is just as good and most professionals use a wire whisk. The most important thing is to resist any temptation to have a high flame. Too much heat will put you into the scrambled egg business. The *sabayon* can be used as a hot sauce over sponge, *choux* paste, or ice-cream. If you want to serve it cold, beat the bowl while it's resting on ice. When the *sabayon* is tepid add a quarter pint of thickly beaten double cream which will help it to stay firm. Some cooks add a little dissolved gelatine but this is cheating. If you do it, deny it.

Index

A la crème (sauce), 99
A la meunière, 168
A la poêle, 185, 197
Agneau, 40–1, 70
Agneau de lait, 70
Agneau de pré-salé, 70
Aigo Bouido, 70
Aiguillette, 70
Aiguillette culotte, 35
Ail, 70
Aioli, 70
Aioli (sauce), 104, 138
Air, 17
Alcohol, 16, 51–60
Allemande (sauce), 100
Aloyau, 35, 70, 188
Andouillettes, 70
Apéritif, 59

Armagnac, 56–7
Arroser, 70
Aspic(s), 70, 134, 199
Aurora (sauce), 99
Aux œufs durs (sauce), 98

Baba au rhum, 70
Bacon, 25, 26
Bain-marie, 70, 93
Baking, 20–1
Ballotine, 175
Bard, 70
Bardes, 48
Bardes de lard, 70
Basting meat, 19
Batter mixture, 144, 160

Bavarian cream, 207
Bavaroise, 206
Bavette, 35
Béarnaise (sauce), 103, 136
Beating, egg-white, 151
Béchamel, 70
Béchamel (sauce), 98, 126
Beef, 34–5
Beef *à la mode*, 184
Beef *mode en gelée*, 184
Beef steaks, 188
Beef suet, 49
Beekenohfe, 70–1
Belly, 38
Best end, 39
Best end of neck, 37, 41

Beurre blanc, 102
Beurre Colbert, 96
Beurre noir, 71
Beurres composés, 71
Bicarbonate of soda, 17
Bifteck, 71
Bifteck à la tartare, 190
Bifteck haché, 71, 190
Bifteck sauté chasseur, 189
Bigarade, 71
Bind, 71
Blade end, 38
Bladebone, 38
Blanc de poulet, 176
Blanch, 71
Blanching, 116, 194
Blanchir, 71, 116